English Magic and
Imperial Madness

CRITICAL EXPLORATIONS IN SCIENCE FICTION AND FANTASY
A series edited by Donald E. Palumbo and C.W. Sullivan III
**Earlier Works:** www.mcfarlandpub.com

57 *Wells Meets Deleuze: The Scientific Romances Reconsidered* (Michael Starr, 2017)

58 *Science Fiction and Futurism: Their Terms and Ideas* (Ace G. Pilkington, 2017)

59 *Science Fiction in Classic Rock: Musical Explorations of Space, Technology and the Imagination, 1967–1982* (Robert McParland, 2017)

60 *Patricia A. McKillip and the Art of Fantasy World-Building* (Audrey Isabel Taylor, 2017)

61 *The Fabulous Journeys of Alice and Pinocchio: Exploring Their Parallel Worlds* (Laura Tosi with Peter Hunt, 2018)

62 *A Dune Companion: Characters, Places and Terms in Frank Herbert's Original Six Novels* (Donald E. Palumbo, 2018)

63 *Fantasy Literature and Christianity: A Study of the Mistborn, Coldfire, Fionavar Tapestry and Chronicles of Thomas Covenant Series* (Weronika Łaszkiewicz, 2018)

64 *The British Comic Invasion: Alan Moore, Warren Ellis, Grant Morrison and the Evolution of the American Style* (Jochen Ecke, 2019)

65 *The Archive Incarnate: The Embodiment and Transmission of Knowledge in Science Fiction* (Joseph Hurtgen, 2018)

66 *Women's Space: Essays on Female Characters in the 21st Century Science Fiction Western* (ed. Melanie A. Marotta, 2019)

67 *"Hailing frequencies open": Communication in Star Trek: The Next Generation* (Thomas D. Parham III, 2019)

68 *The Global Vampire: Essays on the Undead in Popular Culture Around the World* (ed. Cait Coker, 2019)

69 *Philip K. Dick: Essays of the Here and Now* (ed. David Sandner, 2019)

70 *Michael Bishop and the Persistence of Wonder: A Critical Study of the Writings* (Joe Sanders, 2020)

71 *Caitlín R. Kiernan: A Critical Study of Her Dark Fiction* (James Goho, 2020)

72 *In Frankenstein's Wake: Mary Shelley, Morality and Science Fiction* (Alison Bedford, 2020)

73 *The Fortean Influence on Science Fiction: Charles Fort and the Evolution of the Genre* (Tanner F. Boyle, 2020)

74 *Arab and Muslim Science Fiction* (Hosan Elzembely and Emad El-Din Aysha, 2020)

75 *The Mythopoeic Code of Tolkien: A Christian Platonic Reading of the Legendarium* (Jyrki Korpua, 2021)

76 *The Truth of Monsters: Coming of Age with Fantastic Media* (Ildikó Limpár, 2021)

77 *Speculative Modernism: How Science Fiction, Fantasy and Horror Conceived the Twentieth Century* (William Gillard, James Reitter *and* Robert Stauffer, 2021)

78 *English Magic and Imperial Madness: The Anti-Colonial Politics of Susanna Clarke's* Jonathan Strange & Mr. Norrell (Peter D. Mathews, 2021)

# English Magic and Imperial Madness

## The Anti-Colonial Politics of Susanna Clarke's *Jonathan Strange and Mr. Norrell*

PETER D. MATHEWS

CRITICAL EXPLORATIONS IN
SCIENCE FICTION AND FANTASY, 78

*Series Editors* Donald E. Palumbo *and* C.W. Sullivan III

McFarland & Company, Inc., Publishers
*Jefferson, North Carolina*

*This book has undergone peer review.*

ISBN (print) 978-1-4766-8669-1
ISBN (ebook) 978-1-4766-4448-6

LIBRARY OF CONGRESS AND BRITISH LIBRARY
CATALOGUING DATA ARE AVAILABLE

Library of Congress Control Number 2021046627

© 2021 Peter D. Mathews All rights reserved

*No part of this book may be reproduced or transmitted in any form or by any means, electronic or mechanical, including photocopying or recording, or by any information storage and retrieval system, without permission in writing from the publisher.*

Front cover image © 2021 Mia Stendal/Shutterstock

Printed in the United States of America

McFarland & Company, Inc., Publishers
Box 611, Jefferson, North Carolina 28640
*www.mcfarlandpub.com*

For HYUNHEE,
for every reason and every unreason

# Contents

*Acknowledgments* — ix
*Preface* — 1
*Prologue: Merlin's Legacy* — 5
   A Mystic Robe of Midnight Blue — 5
   The Mythological Magician — 9
   Merlin's Imperial Legacy — 15

*Chapter 1. The Fantasy of a Return* — 23
   The Modern Fantasy of Return — 23
   The Englishness of English Magic — 30
   Magic's Persistence — 38

*Chapter 2. Writing, Text, Mythology* — 43
   All the Texts of the World — 43
   The Man Who Was Also a Book — 47
   Writing History, Writing Fiction — 56

*Chapter 3. An Artificial Myth* — 63
   Dual Perspectives — 63
   The English Malady — 69
   Mythologies and Evasions — 76

*Chapter 4. Through the Looking-Glass* — 85
   The Paper Mirror — 85

## Contents

| | |
|---|---|
| THE MONARCH AND THE MIRROR | 90 |
| THE NAMELESS SLAVE | 97 |
| *Chapter 5. Imperialism's Magic Helper* | 105 |
| ANTHROPOLOGY AND UNREASON | 105 |
| THE ILLUSIONIST'S MISSION | 109 |
| THE MAGIC HELPER | 115 |
| *Chapter 6. The Reason of Unreason* | 123 |
| MAGIC AND MADNESS | 123 |
| REASON'S DOUBLE | 126 |
| REASON AND UNREASON | 134 |
| *Epilogue: New Constellations* | 143 |
| THE STARRY HEAVENS | 143 |
| ENDLESS NIGHT | 147 |
| BEYOND DISENCHANTMENT | 150 |
| THE SKY SPEAKS | 153 |
| *References* | 159 |
| *Index* | 165 |

# Acknowledgments

My thanks go to Sean Scarisbrick for reading a very early draft and providing lots of insightful feedback and encouragement that helped me knock the book into shape. I would also like to thank Nicholas Birns for reading a much later draft and convincing me that I really was onto something. You were both instrumental in making the book far better than I ever could have done on my own.

I would also like to thank Nicholas Birns, once again, as well as Robert T. Tally and Jeffrey Weinstock for generously agreeing to read the book and provide blurbs.

I am grateful to the editorial team at McFarland for all their support. Thanks go in particular to Professor C.W. Sullivan III, who recommended this book for inclusion in McFarland's Critical Explorations in Science Fiction and Fantasy series, and Susan Kilby, for all her editorial assistance.

As always, the most important person I have to thank is my wife, Hyunhee Shin. She provides the love and support that makes my work possible. I write best when I feel loved and happy, so it is no surprise that the time since we met and fell in love has coincided with the most prolific period of my career. Hyunhee, you are my everything, and that is why this book is dedicated to you.

# Preface

This book is a study of the intertwining themes of madness and magic in the novel *Jonathan Strange and Mr. Norrell* (2004) by the English author Susanna Clarke. What drew me to this project was an intuition that, beneath the surface of Clarke's idiosyncratic and brilliant fantasy novel, there lies a complex historical and cultural critique of English imperialism. The idea that modern England has been indelibly shaped by a colonial past with which it has never truly come to terms has been highlighted by recent scholarly studies. Padraic X. Scanlan's *Slave Empire: How Slavery Built Modern Britain* (2020) and Sathnam Sanghera's *Empireland: How Imperialism Has Shaped Modern Britain* (2021), for instance, show not only how the wealth stolen from its colonies shaped England economically, but also how the disavowed brutality of that plunder continues to affect its moral and psychological self-image. "Nostalgia for the British empire gains traction from the idea that British imperialism was fundamentally commercial, and therefore benign," writes Scanlan. "The revival of free trade on the imperial model is a part of the fantasy of a post–Brexit Britain" (Scanlan, 2020, p. 27). This willful amnesia must be understood as part of a larger thematic web in Clarke's novel, in which the issue of imperialism is both invisible and ubiquitous.

The symbolic threads that run more discernibly through *Jonathan Strange and Mr. Norrell* are magic and madness, two terms that are connected by the fact that insanity, with the sole exception of Norrell, serves as the precondition for the attainment of magical powers. This is true not only of fairies, who possess a malicious reputation for thinking in unreasonable ways, but also their associates, the Aureate magicians. It is by learning from these precursors, for instance, that Strange, who chooses deliberately to go mad, enhances his magical abilities. Magic provides the magician not only with access to power through the act

## Preface

of enchantment, but also to people with authority and influence who wish to direct that magic to their own ends. Magic has a long history as a moral allegory for the way that power corrupts, sometimes to the point of insanity, those who wield it. Alongside the numerous monarchs driven mad by power, therefore, there is an abundance of magicians in the English literary tradition, from Faustus to Manfred, who have likewise tumbled over the brink of sanity.

How, then, does this rich imaginative history of mad magicians connect to the history of English imperialism? The answer lies in the legitimizing power of myth, a tradition that begins with the figure of Merlin, whose legacy is the necessary starting point for this study. Not only does Merlin gain magical powers through the agency of madness, but he uses those powers to place Arthur on the throne. "Arthurian romance, at the outset, collaborates with medieval Europe's earliest project of overseas empire," observes Geraldine Heng in *Empire of Magic: Medieval Romance and the Politics of Cultural Fantasy* (Heng, 2003, p. 5). Since the twelfth century, the legend of Merlin has been used to justify the English claim to power, culminating in the Elizabethan court magician John Dee's assertion that the British Empire—a term he coined—was simply a reclamation of the ancient territories once ruled by Arthur. Residing at the historical intersection of magic, madness, and imperialism is the vexing question of how power is deployed and legitimated, a theme that finds repeated expression in English literature, from Edmund Spenser's *The Faerie Queene* (1590–96) to A.S. Byatt's *The Virgin in the Garden* (1978). Placing *Jonathan Strange and Mr. Norrell* in this larger context reveals the extent to which Clarke's novel is also decisively shaped by this history, a cultural tradition from which she simultaneously draws inspiration and criticizes for its ethical failures. The primary goal of *English Magic and Imperial Madness*, therefore, is to equip the reader with the necessary historical and cultural background to engage in an informed reading of the book's political critique of English imperialism.

Apart from *Jonathan Strange and Mr. Norrell*, Clarke has published two other books—*The Ladies of Grace Adieu*, a collection of short stories that appeared in 2006, and a second novel, *Piranesi*, published in 2020—each of which deals with themes of magic and madness. Even though they are not analyzed extensively in *English Magic and Imperial Madness*, these works provide valuable supplements to my reading

*Preface*

of Clarke's first novel. The title story of *The Ladies of Grace Adieu*, for instance, presents a very different perspective on the Strange/Norrell universe, in which magic is secretly practiced with cool rationality by three women of varying classes, in pointed contrast to the often hysterical drama of Clarke's two upper-class, male magicians. *Piranesi*, likewise, deploys magical rituals in Clarke's description of the passage between this world and the House, while Piranesi's disjointed recollection of his former self raises persistent questions about the meaning of sanity. The strange world of the House slowly acquires an aura of wisdom and warm familiarity when seen through the eyes of Piranesi, in pointed contrast to the alienating chaos of the modern world that confronts him when he resumes his life as Matthew Rose Sorensen.

What distinguishes *Jonathan Strange and Mr. Norrell* from these other treatments of magic and madness is its insistence on placing these themes in the context of English history and culture. Clarke's decision to set her novel during the Napoleonic Wars of the early nineteenth century, for instance, is a strategic one. Her skillful pastiche of nineteenth-century literary and historical discourses requires the reader to reconsider not only this pivotal period, but also to inquire into a deeper past that, for all its fictional improvisations, is evidently drawn from the permutations of English history. To read *Jonathan Strange and Mr. Norrell* without understanding this context has frequently led, as Nicholas Birns contends, to wrong "assumptions that the book is nostalgic for a sovereign magic, when in fact its historicity is a way of shaking up time itself" (Birns, 2020, p. 125). *English Magic and Imperial Madness* allows future readers to gain a fuller understanding of the ethical vision that underpins Clarke's groundbreaking novel, one that interweaves the twin themes of magic and madness to challenge the moral failings produced by England's imperial legacy.

# Prologue: Merlin's Legacy

## A Mystic Robe of Midnight Blue

As a fantasy novel, Susanna Clarke's *Jonathan Strange and Mr. Norrell* is inevitably framed by a set of expectations, as evidenced by the immediate reactions to its publication, which recognize Clarke's adherence to the parameters of the genre while simultaneously acknowledging the extent to which she twists and undermines them for her own ends. In his review in *The New York Times*, for instance, John Hodgman presents the book as the logical product of an increasingly successful overlap between literary and genre fiction. "Fantasy has not, of course, been absent from literary fiction, but it has been admitted to the mainstream generally only when pedigreed (Martin Amis's *Time's Arrow*), political (Margaret Atwood's *Handmaid's Tale*) or exotic (which is to say, Latin American)," writes Hodgman. "Fantasy and science fiction as a capital G genre, meanwhile, has largely been shelved separately from the rest of the culture, [...] [but] it is hard to deny a sense that the boundaries between genre and literary fiction are slipping" (Hodgman, 2004). Michael Dirda reflects similarly on how Clarke's novel places itself within the tradition of English fantasy carved out by Mervyn Peake, T.H. White, and J.R.R. Tolkien, while at the same time demonstrating an intellectual depth that is typical of literary fiction. "Her antiquarian romance more accurately resembles Umberto Eco's *Foucault's Pendulum*, Lawrence Norfolk's *Lemprière's Dictionary* and John Crowley's *Aegypt* sequence—deeply learned novels that reimagine the nature of history," observes Dirda (Dirda, 2004). The fantasy elements of *Jonathan Strange and Mr. Norrell* thus provide the novel with its engagement with English magic, on the one hand, while its literary dimensions offer a sophisticated consideration of the history of English imperialism on the other.

## Prologue: Merlin's Legacy

This willingness to transgress the boundaries of genre reflects the playful quality of Clarke's novel, which lures in the reader through the recurrent misdirection of its intentions. For instance, one of the most obvious ways that a magician can be identified is by their physical appearance, yet Clarke subverts this expectation from the outset. Norrell is the first magician the reader encounters in *Jonathan Strange and Mr. Norrell*, a fastidious and unremarkable gentleman from Yorkshire whose misanthropy habitually confines him to his library. Beneath this scholarly mien, however, there is a hunger for power that eventually sees him employed by the highest echelons of the government. During his initial reluctant forays into London social life, Norrell is forced to endure a number of tiresome parties, to which he is invited because of the stories circulating about his magical feat of making the stones speak at York Minster. At one such event, he happens to overhear a guest proclaim loudly that Norrell "is never to be seen without a mystic robe of midnight blue, adorned with otherlandish symbols!" (Clarke, 2015, p. 56). Clearly, this braggart has never seen Norrell with their own eyes, for this description could not be more wrong. Where did this received idea of how a magician should look come from? The answer is to be found in the legendary figure of Merlin, the great wizard from the Arthurian stories, whose historical significance implicitly frames Clarke's novel.

As it turns out, Norrell is the exception that proves the rule, for the other key magicians portrayed in the novel do, in general, follow the external characteristics that are expected of them. After Norrell, the next magician the reader meets is Vinculus, a dirty street magician whose booth is located in Threadneedle-street, opposite the Bank of England. When Vinculus shows up uninvited in Norrell's library, Clarke describes him in the following manner:

> Mr Norrell looked up and was astonished to find that there was someone else in the room, a person he had never seen before, a thin, shabby, ragged hawk of a man. His face was the colour of three-day-old milk; his hair was the colour of a coal-smoke-and-ashes London sky; and his clothes were the colour of the Thames at dirty Wapping. Nothing about him—face, hair, clothes—was particularly clean, but in all other points he corresponded to the common notion of what a magician should look like (which Mr Norrell most certainly did not) [Clarke, 2015, pp. 149–150].

## Prologue: Merlin's Legacy

Vinculus's appearance is the epitome of the local cunning-man, a purveyor of charms, spells, and other low enchantments that the general public in London associates with the word "magic." That Norrell looks nothing like Vinculus is no accident: his attire is a reflection not only of his social and financial status, but his stated desire to create a modern and respectable form of English magic.

Norrell and Vinculus represent the opposite ends of magic's social continuum, the split between high and low that will be explored more deeply in Chapter 1. Despite their connection to the world of the occult, these two magicians are portrayed as uninspiring, disenchanted, even repellent characters. The powers they wield stand in stark contrast to their lack of personal charm and persuasion, creating a jarring disjunction between power and its appearance. These two varieties of modern magician are juxtaposed in *Jonathan Strange and Mr. Norrell* to what might be called the "mythological magician," a figure whose magical abilities are mirrored by an outward appearance that charms and seduces. Strange fits perfectly this second set of expectations. "Strange was everyone's idea of what a magician ought to be," writes Clarke. "He was tall; he was charming; he had a most ironical smile; and, unlike Mr Norrell, he talked a great deal about magic and had no objection to answering any body's questions on the subject" (Clarke, 2015, p. 328).

The modern magician in Norrell harbors a sense of ambition that leads him, for instance, to seek out an alliance with the politician Sir Walter Pole, to participate in the war against the French, and to argue for the re-establishment of a legal system for regulating magic in the form of the Cinque Dragownes, among other things. In short, Norrell uses his magic to gain access to the non-magical mechanisms of the state, which he then deploys to compel others into following his vision for modern magic. This strategy is shown to be effective, but it comes with a major drawback: the high-handed and coercive manner in which Norrell exercises his power makes him universally disliked. A key aspect of the persona of the mythological magician, by contrast, is the seductive power of their charm. Power comes so easily to them that it can seem effortless, a kind of natural genius. When Norrell is initially recruited for the war effort, for instance, the commanding officer, Captain Harcourt-Bruce, imagines a heroic figure like the Raven King coming to the aid of his troops. Harcourt-Bruce is himself something of a romantic archetype, good-looking and courageous, and the news of the return of English

## Prologue: Merlin's Legacy

magic inspires in him visions of gallant skirmishes straight out of the pages of a Walter Scott novel, in which the Raven King rides at the head of his fairy horde to reinforce the English armies. Harcourt-Bruce's fantasy of what a magician should look like is commensurate with this dramatic scenario, and so it is that he is let down by the decidedly unheroic figure of Norrell (Clarke, 2015, pp. 125–126). Norrell never makes it to the battlefield, of course, since through a mixture of cowardice and greed he arranges for Strange to go in his place. Strange is thus packed off to Portugal, under the command of Lord Wellington, where he is given a meaningful nickname—Merlin, after the greatest mythological magician of them all.

Merlin is only mentioned a handful of times in *Jonathan Strange and Mr. Norrell*, but his influence is pervasive. The first reference comes early in the novel, at a London party where Norrell is being asked about the Raven King. Mrs. Littlefield expresses her astonishment at Norrell's indifference to that figure. "I never met a magician yet who did not declare that the Black King was the greatest of them all—the magician par excellence!" she exclaims. "A man who could, had he so desired, have wrested Merlin from the tree, spun the old gentleman on his head and put him back in again" (Clarke, 2015, p. 70). In a footnote, Clarke observes that the Raven King, who is also known as John Uskglass, was the one who brought magic back to England after the disappearance of Merlin. "The Raven King was not the first British magician. There had been others before him—notably the seventh-century half-man, half-demon, Merlin—but at the time the Raven King came into England there were none" (Clarke, 2015, p. 282). In a later footnote, the reader is told how there is a long tradition of magicians learning from dead predecessors—the Raven King, for instance, was said to have consulted with such legendary figures as the Witch of Endor, Moses and his brother Aaron, Joseph of Arimathea, and of course, Merlin himself (Clarke, 2015, p. 688). Another notable reference comes from Strange's review of Portishead's book, in which Strange contemplates why the Norrellite position rejects the legacy of earlier magicians. In the case of Merlin, he argues, since Merlin's mother was Welsh and his father was reputed to be a succubus, people like Portishead and Norrell have excluded him mainly on moral grounds, for such a figure hardly appeals to the kind of bourgeois, respectable audience they are trying to persuade of the value of modern English magic. What is more, points out Strange, unlike the

*Prologue: Merlin's Legacy*

Raven King, Merlin had no known disciples or followers, and thus he did not leave behind the same kind of legacy (Clarke, 2015, p. 530). So writes the magician who, when Lord Wellington addresses him, answers to the name "Merlin" and, in so doing, puts on the "mystic robe of midnight blue" (Clarke, 2015, p. 56) of the mythological magician.

## *The Mythological Magician*

Merlin is a character born from myth, a magical figure whose personal story is entangled with the history of England through the Arthurian legends. The Merlin with which most readers are familiar today, however, is the product of an obsessive process of rewriting. Merlin first entered into the English popular imagination through Geoffrey of Monmouth's wildly inaccurate chronicle *The History of the Kings of Britain*, but his story has repeatedly been embellished and reworked over the centuries. In the fifteenth century, for instance, Merlin's legend was famously retold in Thomas Malory's *Le Morte d'Arthur* (1485), one of the most influential versions of the Arthurian legend. The more tragic aspects of Merlin's story are highlighted in Tennyson's poem "Merlin and Vivien" (1859), from his Arthurian cycle *Idylls of the King*, which tells how Vivien, the Lady of the Lake, seduced Merlin and then used magic to imprison him in an oak tree—this is the incident to which Mrs. Littlefield is referring in her conversation at the party with Norrell. Merlin's modern metamorphosis is made complete with T.H. White's *The Sword in the Stone* (1938), in which his more dangerous aspects (such as his demonic parenthood) are removed, transforming him into a wise and warm-hearted mentor to Arthur. These examples represent only a few of the thousands of variations of the Merlin myth, a story that has been adapted to mirror the emotional and political needs of each period in which it has been retold. The significant echoes of Merlin's legacy in *Jonathan Strange and Mr. Norrell* mean that Clarke's novel, too, may be regarded as a permutation of this legend.

The repeated appropriation of Merlin to serve various political purposes, as Strange notes, has tended to obscure his Welsh origins. This process begins, in fact, with Geoffrey of Monmouth, who inserts Merlin into his story of the kings of Britain. Geoffrey does not conceal the fact that he is drawing from Welsh mythology in writing about this

## Prologue: Merlin's Legacy

character—indeed, in order to circumvent charges of heresy or subversion, Geoffrey officially denies authorship of *The History of the Kings of Britain*, claiming instead that he merely transcribed its contents from ancient Welsh sources. One of the first people to question the integrity of Geoffrey of Monmouth's account was the historian Gerald of Wales. Gerald highlights, in particular, the way that Geoffrey, in recreating the character of Merlin, takes two separate figures from Welsh mythology and combines them into a single entity:

> There were two Merlins. The one called Ambrosius, who thus had two names, prophesied when Vortigern was King. He was the son of an incubus and he was discovered in Carmarthen, which means Merlin's town, for it takes its name from the fact that he was found there. The second Merlin came from Scotland. He is called Celidonius, because he prophesied in the Calidonian Forest. He is also called Silvester, because once when he was fighting he looked up into the air and saw a terrible monster. He went mad as a result and fled to the forest where he passed the remainder of his life as a wild man of the woods. This second Merlin lived in the time of Arthur. He is said to have made more prophecies than his namesake [Wales, 2004, p. 192].

The figure of Merlin that emerges from Geoffrey of Monmouth's chronicle is therefore actually a composite of earlier mythical figures. Even his name has been changed from its Celtic form "Myrddin" to "Merlin"—probably because the former, to Norman ears, would have sounded too close to the French word "*merde*," meaning "shit."

The Welsh version of Merlin, whom Gerald refers to as "Meilyr," anticipates various aspects of Clarke's book. In an echo of Vinculus's prophecy about the advent of two magicians, for instance, Gerald relates how "at a time when the kingdom of Britain still existed, the two Merlins, Celidonius and Ambrosius, each foretold its destruction, and the coming first of the Saxons and then of the Normans" (Wales, 2004, p. 247). The most important part of Gerald's story, however, is the tale of how Merlin acquired his magical powers:

> It is worth relating that in our days there lived [...] a certain Welshman called Meilyr who could explain the occult and foretell the future. He acquired his skill in the following way. One evening, and, to be precise, it was Palm Sunday, he happened to meet a girl whom he had loved for a long time. She was very beautiful, the spot was an attractive one, and it seemed too good an opportunity to be missed. He was enjoying himself

in her arms and tasting her delights, when suddenly, instead of the beautiful girl, he found in his embrace a hairy creature, rough and shaggy, and, indeed, repulsive beyond words. As he stared at the monster his wits deserted him and he became quite mad. He remained in this condition for many years. Eventually he recovered his health in the church of St David's, thanks to the virtues of the saintly men of that place. All the same, he retained a very close and most remarkable familiarity with unclean spirits, being able to see them, recognizing them, talking to them and calling them each by his own name, so that with their help he could often prophesy the future [Wales, 2004, pp. 116–117].

Just like Strange's experiments with induced madness in *Jonathan Strange and Mr. Norrell*, Merlin's powers are a result of his excursion into the realm of insanity, where he learns from "unclean spirits" (fairies) how to deploy his magic. Merlin thus establishes the crucial connection between madness and magic that proves so central to the story of Strange, who is known as "Merlin" among his military friends.

The parallel between the madness of Strange and Merlin creates a further tie to Welsh mythology. Ancient Welsh culture possessed the distinctive notion of *"awen,"* the practitioners of which Gerald of Wales portrays in his book *The Description of Wales*. "Among the Welsh there are certain individuals called *'awenyddion'* who behave as if they are possessed by devils," he writes. "They do not answer the question put to them in any logical way. Words stream from their mouths, incoherently and apparently meaningless and without any sense at all, but all the same well expressed: and if you listen carefully to what they say you will receive the solution to your problem" (Wales, 2004, p. 246). The significance of this peculiar form of insanity has received much attention from critics and historians of medieval culture. In "The Nature of Prophecy in Geoffrey of Monmouth's *Vita Merlini*" (1990), for instance, Jan Ziolkowski explains that the "word *awenyddion* is the plural of *awenydd*, a word that means poet-prophet and that derives from *awen* ('in-spiration') 'oracular frenzy'" (Ziolkowski, 1990, p. 242). In the introduction to their new translation of *The Book of Taliesin*, Gwyneth Lewis and Rowan Williams distinguish *awen* from similar cultural phenomena, such as the ancient Greek idea of poetic inspiration. "It would be misleading to translate this idea of inspiration as 'Muse,'" they write, "it is better thought of as a state of altered consciousness in which the poet receives knowledge of matters beyond what can be routinely learned"

## Prologue: Merlin's Legacy

(Taliesin, 2019, p. xxv). As such, both Merlin (or Myrddin) and the magic inspired by *awen* are originally rooted specifically in Welsh medieval culture.

The combination of these earlier mythical figures into a single person by Geoffrey of Monmouth is not, therefore, a negligible change. The key transformation that takes place with *The History of the Kings of England* is an uprooting of Merlin/Myrddin from his historical and cultural roots, a displacement that allows this character to be rewritten and adapted, over and over again, in the service of different causes. For this reason, Anne Lawrence-Mathers, in her study *The True History of Merlin the Magician* (2012), emphasizes the enormity of the split between these two manifestations of the Merlin story. "Merlin the magician, like his name, was a creation of the twelfth century," she insists. "This is no attempt to deny the existence of earlier Welsh sources, but Myrddin the princely bard of the Cymry, driven mad by a disastrous battle and expressing himself in cryptic poetry, needs to be separated from the twelfth-century Merlin" (Lawrence-Mathers, 2012, p. 15). Geoffrey's Merlin is such a dramatic reinvention that, despite recycling names and events from ancient Welsh sources, his version must be seen as an attempt to create something radically new and different.

The first thing to note about Geoffrey of Monmouth's Merlin is how, particularly in comparison to his ancient precursors, he has been updated to fit the values of the twelfth century. This phenomenon is already familiar to modern readers from period dramas and historical novels, which often feature characters wearing historically accurate clothing who nonetheless speak and act in ways that are wholly anachronistic. While the almost nine centuries that separate today's reader from Geoffrey's work make this disparity more difficult to detect, to the medieval scholar the recasting of the ancient Merlin in contemporary terms is nonetheless striking:

> Geoffrey of Monmouth's Merlin was both boy wizard and the magus of the twelfth-century renaissance. [...] This historical Merlin was an embodiment of all the major types of magician: a seer, an inspired prophet, an astrologer, a proto-alchemist, an expert in natural magic, and an adept in cosmology. He also had the unique advantage of having no need to summon demons to work his magic, since he was himself the son of a demon (whilst also being a Christian). He was no figure from folklore or the creation of popular tradition: he embodied the cutting edge of

## Prologue: Merlin's Legacy

mediaeval science, and his powers were convincingly real. This needs to be understood: Merlin's powers and prophecies, which appear so obviously fantastical—if not nonsensical—to a modern audience, were taken wholly seriously [Lawrence-Mathers, 2012, p. 6].

The twelfth and thirteenth centuries were a time of intellectual revival in England, epitomized by the founding of the universities at Oxford and Cambridge. While disciplines like magic and alchemy would be out of place in today's academic culture, they were crucial drivers in the historical and intellectual development of English culture.

At this time, England also started to cultivate a new and deeper sense of its national identity through the work of historians like Geoffrey of Monmouth. Indeed, this capacity of the myth of Merlin to have a material impact on history is another key feature of this character. In the Arthurian legends, Merlin is responsible for putting the fabled king on the throne and so launching the Arthurian legend, but his legacy goes far beyond that. That is because Geoffrey, by retelling the story of Merlin, helped to transform the narrative of England from that of a small backwater on the margins of Europe, to the story of a mythical superpower that, despite falling into decline after its Arthurian glory days, promises to rise again one day.

> Merlin's powers and prophecies, which appear so obviously fantastical [...] were taken wholly seriously. They even helped to add credibility to the "long-lost" history which first revealed them to a wide European public. Merlin, therefore, quite literally helped to change history, and in particular he helped to put British history into world history, from which it had largely been excluded. The twelfth and thirteenth centuries produced a great outburst of scholarly and literary activity, with the writing of history playing a key role in expressing a new understanding of the world. [...] [Geoffrey of Monmouth] provided an origin story for the inhabitants of Britain, tracing them back to the survivors of fallen Troy, and putting them on a par with the Romans (who claimed descent from Aeneas) as well as all the new, post–Roman nations who were claiming similar Trojan ancestry. In the process, the history of Britain was explicitly correlated with biblical and classical history, to take its place on a world stage [Lawrence-Mathers, 2012, pp. 6–7].

Geoffrey thus creates a new historical narrative for England that dazzles readers with its heroism and renown, awakening admiration by

## Prologue: Merlin's Legacy

depicting an invented past that, while being demonstrably untrue, can nonetheless be used to arouse new aspirations to greatness where none existed before. This kind of history is thus, in a sense, a form of magic, creating a future reality through the power of the imagination.

Geoffrey of Monmouth showed how a mythological story could be used to rewrite the past and, in the process, compose a new future for England. Certainly, his heroic vision of England's past provided a more enticing alternative than its most famous precursors, Gildas's *The Ruin of Britain* and Bede's *Ecclesiastical History of the English People*. While these accounts maintained their historical authority among scholars, Geoffrey's success came from the way his chronicle tapped into the new intellectual and political conditions of the twelfth century. Bede shows England exiting the stage of world history with the departure of the Romans, while Gildas portrays "the decline of the British" as "a story of wickedness and stupidity receiving predictable punishment," whereas Geoffrey "turned the Britons back into the heroes of their own story" (Lawrence-Mathers, 2012, p. 41). Geoffrey's rewriting of the English monarchy also had a more direct impetus, arriving in the wake of a succession crisis that followed the death of Henry I, the last of the Norman kings. Henry's daughter Matilda would have been next in line for the throne, but his nephew Stephen of Blois instead seized power for himself. Geoffrey's revision of the historical record proved to be the perfect antidote to this period of instability:

> The writing of history always has a political dimension, but this was especially true when the conquering Norman dynasty was in danger of disintegrating. The 1130s were a time of the potential fall (and rise) of dynasties, when any insight into the future would be welcome—especially in England. [...] When Stephen of Blois broke his oath to accept Matilda as queen, and had himself crowned king of England in 1135, the search for both an acceptable explanation of the present and some insight into the future became even more pressing. Moreover, any such analysis had to be addressed to a political class which had changed radically since 1066. The Anglo-Norman aristocracy in no way identified with the Anglo-Saxon past. There was also a new interest in the writing of dynastic and national histories. Both political and intellectual developments therefore led to a pressing need for new accounts of "British" history and new ways of understanding the current situation. [...] Geoffrey's *History* thus filled an urgent gap, whilst Merlin's prophecies

*Prologue: Merlin's Legacy*

offered information (however hard to interpret) on the future of Britain [Lawrence-Mathers, 2012, pp. 23–25].

Geoffrey's chronicle helped to establish the legitimacy of King Stephen by rewriting the royal past in his favor. Yet the true impact of the *History* came from the way it reshaped Britain's future. Merlin was accepted as a real-life prophet and magician until the seventeenth century, while the popularity of Geoffrey's book meant that its perspective was disseminated far and wide as a historically accurate account for four hundred years.

## Merlin's Imperial Legacy

The true legacy of Merlin in *Jonathan Strange and Mr. Norrell* thus lies not so much in the romantic stereotypes of the magician to which Captain Harcourt-Bruce or Jonathan Strange subscribe—the flowing beard, for instance, or the long robes and wizard's hat—but in the mythical creation of an England that is rooted, on one side, in a past that values heroism and virtue, and on the other, in a future, a manifest destiny that promises greatness and imperial glory. Indeed, there is a powerful sense in which the two sides of this emerging mythology mirror each other, grounded in the assumption that it is *because* the English are heroic and virtuous that they are destined to be wise and benevolent rulers over their subjects. Even after people stopped believing that Merlin was a real person, his legend continued to provide a point of inspiration for English national myths—he turns up again in this role, for instance, in Edmund Spenser's *Faerie Queene*, in which it is now the Tudor family that is seeking to consolidate its royal legitimacy.

Merlin's role as a prophet also affirmed the soothing idea that the future greatness of England was, if not yet present, always on the horizon, while his rootless, timeless aspects as a mythological figure meant that these prophecies were infinitely adaptable. Geoffrey of Monmouth's much darker portrait in *The Life of Merlin* explores this visionary side of Merlin's character. Lawrence-Mathers argues that these prophecies are especially important for how they shift the national mythology away from England and instead highlight the more abstract notion of Britain:

## Prologue: Merlin's Legacy

> Merlin's prophecies [...] raised political and theological issues of enormous importance. Thus kings, courtiers, churchmen and scholars all paid attention; and questions of interpretation were taken very seriously. When the great prophecies were revealed in the 1130s, no reader could have missed the fact that Merlin was a political prophet. [...] This has the rather counterfactual effect of giving the idea of Britain a status far higher than that of England—even though England existed as a political reality in the mediaeval period, and Britain did not. [...] This gives the kings of Britain something of the status of figures in the moral fables and legendary stories with which twelfth-century readers would have been familiar from their school days. It was also an innovation in prophetic language, since neither biblical nor classical prophets had used such imagery in quite this way [Lawrence-Mathers, 2012, p. 72].

Geoffrey's rewriting of the Merlin myth thus provides a new and heroic vision of what it means to be English, one that draws together the medieval academic disciplines of magic and brings them into the service of an emerging political ideology, one that will later prove crucial to the development of England's imperial ambitions.

Nowhere is Merlin's imperial legacy clearer than the case of the Elizabethan polymath and magician John Dee. Clarke does not mention Dee in the course of *Jonathan Strange and Mr. Norrell*, but there are indications that he is, at least in part, the model for her fictional character Dr. Gregory Absalom. In Clarke's novel, Absalom was the creator of the Shadow House, an important magical location in England, and the place where Strange first encounters Segundus and Honeyfoot. One of the main hints tying Absalom to Dee is Clarke's observation that Norrell is the first magician that the English government has employed in two hundred years, with Absalom having been the last person to have held that position (Clarke, 2015, p. 123). Clarke relates that Absalom had a long career as the court magician to Henry VIII, Mary I, and Elizabeth I, a position that Dee also held during the time of Elizabeth (Clarke, 2015, pp. 266–267). The political tensions between England and France during the Elizabethan period resulted in a magical arms race, with Dee on one side and his French rival, Nostradamus, on the other. This situation is replicated in Clarke's novel when, after Norrell joins the war effort, Napoleon attempts, fruitlessly, to recruit a magician for the French side (Clarke, 2015, p. 135). Dee's enormous library, meanwhile, which dwarfed those of both Cambridge and Oxford at the time, resembles the collection put together by Norrell. Dee certainly knew the stories of Merlin and Arthur—indeed, included in his library was a folio copy of Merlin's prophecies by Geoffrey of Monmouth, complete with commentary and illustrations. In many Arthurian legends, Merlin is presented as the magical protector of England, casting spells that bring down destruction on its enemies. In *Jonathan Strange and Mr. Norrell*, the reader witnesses both Norrell and Strange undertaking similar defensive tasks, from a decoy composed of ships made out of rain, to magical shields placed along the southern border to repel intruders. In his own time, Dee played a similar role, most famously when England was threatened by the Spanish Armada in 1588. Dee "offered counsel when the Spanish Armada threatened the country, predicting its destruction by storms. When his prediction came true, there were some who said the wizard had conjured up the storms himself" (Carr-Gomm & Heygate, 2010, p. 260). In a society where magic was taken seriously, Dee's reputation as a defender of the nation, in the tradition of Merlin, was no small thing.

The Elizabethan era was marked by this kind of intense self-mythologizing—Frances A. Yates, for instance, devoted an entire book to this theme, examining, in particular, the recurrent comparison of Elizabeth I to the Greek goddess Astraea. Astraea was the goddess of wisdom and innocence, whose virginal status is reflected in her eventual transformation, upon abandoning the human world, into the constellation Virgo. When Virgil writes in the fourth *Eclogue* that when "Justice returns to earth, the Golden Age returns" (Virgil, 2009, p. 18), the English translation of "Justice" obscures the fact that the Latin original is actually "Astraea." The fabled return of Astraea appears repeatedly in English literature—Spenser refers to it in *The Faerie Queene*, for instance, while John Dryden celebrates the restoration of Charles II to the English throne in 1660 with his poem "Astraea Redux," which bears Virgil's line as its epigraph (Dryden, 2001, p. 11). Yates observes "that from the very beginning of her reign the Virgo-Astraea symbol was used of Elizabeth" (Yates, 1975, p. 59), an act of self-mythologization designed to portend an English golden age. As such, the victory over the Spanish Armada was more than a military victory, it was also an affirmation that this prophecy had come true:

> Elizabeth's victory over the Spanish Armada was a victory, not only over a national enemy, but also over a spiritual power which made a total

## Prologue: Merlin's Legacy

> claim on men's allegiance. To defeat it required not only a strong navy but also a strong symbolism. By claiming for the national church that it was a reform executed by the sacred imperial power as represented in the sacred English monarchy, the Elizabeth symbol drew to itself a tradition which also made a total, a universal claim—the tradition of sacred empire. [...] Through these associations, the imperial theme in relation to Queen Elizabeth has overtones which soar beyond the individual destinies of the Tudors and their realm. [...] The unmarried state of the Queen is exalted into a symbol of the imperial virgin Astraea which fills the universe [Yates, 1975, pp. 58–59].

The historic defeat of the Spanish Armada is subsequently overlaid by mythological symbols borrowed from competing traditions, drawing together the Greek goddess Astraea and the legendary Arthurian figure of Merlin, whose combined powers demonstrate the providential superiority of the Protestant god over that of the Catholic Spanish. The history of how England mythologizes itself is replete with such borrowed glories, which are replicated and repurposed to its own ends, much as Clarke is doing in her novel.

This myth-making practice takes on even greater significance in the emerging conception of a British Empire, an idea that was first meaningfully articulated by Dee, the Merlin of Elizabeth's court.* The English monarchy needed gold to finance its military ambitions, and its logic in appointing Dee lay in the hope that his skills in the field of alchemy might provide them with an abundant new source of wealth. While Dee failed in this alchemical mission, he nonetheless identified a different, non-magical stream of revenue that was to prove far more lucrative. "Upon Mary's death, Elizabeth [...] ascended to the throne, marking the opening of one of the most culturally and militarily expansive periods of English history," writes Jason Louv in *John Dee and the Empire of Angels* (2018). "Elizabeth would soon implement Dee's work in naval strategy and optics to transition England into an empire. Dee would later come to compare himself and Elizabeth to Merlin and King Arthur, respectively—even suggesting that they were the reincarnations of that legendary syzygy" (Louv, 2018, p. 82). Dee subsequently fell from

---

*Bruce Ward Henry points out that the term "British Empire" was actually first used by the Welsh historian Humphrey Llwyd. While this may technically be true, Dee's vision for what that might entail and how to implement it is what gives the term its longstanding substance (Henry, 1972, p. 189).

## Prologue: Merlin's Legacy

grace, his reputation ruined by accusations of sorcery, but his ideas were crucial in changing the history not just of England, but of the world.

Dee was such a pivotal figure because he "provided the ideological underpinning for the concept of the British Empire," and he "was the first person to use that term" (Carr-Gomm & Heygate, 2010, p. 260). Yet Dee's role was not only theoretical: in the 1570s his knowledge of maps and navigation was instrumental in England taking its initial steps toward building an empire. Dee was the driving force behind Francis Drake's circumnavigation of the tip of South America in 1579, for instance, the first practical move toward colonization. The success of the Spanish in amassing a huge amount of silver from their colonies, along with a concurrent decline in the English economy, was the financial impetus behind this strategy:

> It is in this context that Dee gave the world the concept of a "British Empire," a phrase he coined. After Columbus's discovery of the New World, Pope Alexander VI had divided the Americas between Portugal and Spain in the Treaty of Tordesillas, handing them dominion over the Atlantic. Dee, with his back pocket full of superior knowledge of geography, navigation, and optics, would soon suggest Elizabeth contest this, and expand into the New World not just to rival Catholic domination, but for economic growth. Dee's knowledge of optics, as well as the geographic and cartographic information he had absorbed under Mercator and his other mentors, at a time when accurate cartographic information was largely confined to the Continent, made him invaluable in not only conceptualizing but actualizing this plan [Louv, 2018, pp. 127–128].

The English were successful in creating a worldwide empire, beginning with the establishment of the Virginia colony (named after Elizabeth, the "Virgin Queen") in 1607, and expanding rapidly through the nineteenth century, so that by the beginning of World War I almost a quarter of the world was under British rule.

The long history of voracious greed and brutal exploitation that marks the rise and fall of the British Empire tends to draw the attention of most historians to the economic and political motives that underpinned its formation. While such a disenchanted focus is understandable, it should not obscure the religious and magical motives that were also at play. In the early modern period, there was a growing expectation that the biblical end-times predicted in the Book of Revelation were

## Prologue: Merlin's Legacy

imminent. Rather than seeing Dee's contributions to the development of the British Empire and his conversations with angels as separate activities, they should instead be understood as corresponding aspects of a single project, joined together by his eschatological outlook. Louv, for instance, emphasizes this religious connection in the writing of Dee's influential book *General and Rare Memorials Pertayning to the Perfect Arte of Navigation* (1577):

> In November 1577, Dee presented a new imperial plan to Elizabeth, suggesting that England wrest control of the New World from Spain— *General and Rare Memorials*, a set of documents laying out plans and technical guidelines for a new era of English colonization. The *Memorials* continued the occult inquiry Dee began in the *Propaedeumata aphoristica* and *Monas hieroglyphica;* as with those books, Dee thought the *Memorials* divinely inspired (also by the angel Michael, in the case of the *Monas*). For Dee, the *Memorials* were a revelation from the angels, divine guidance on the creating of a British Empire, through a Royal Navy that would hold the world in its sway [Louv, 2018, pp. 130–131].

Dee's plan would "establish Elizabeth as the world ruler before the end times arrived," a political culmination that would be paralleled, in turn, by a magical one, the establishment of "a new alchemical institute to produce the philosopher's stone—the final perfection of which would reestablish the empire in full" (Louv, 2018, p. 131). The peculiar logic behind this strategy, Yates explains in *The Occult Philosophy in the Elizabeth Age* (1979), was to make "the world worthy" of Christ's return, "which would hasten its advent" (Yates, 2001, p. 216).

This religious mythology is reinforced, in turn, by a new national mythology that Dee forges from the Arthurian legends. The story of Arthur was useful to Dee for the way it recast the English imperial adventure not as an aggressive political strategy designed to outstrip their Spanish arch-rivals, but as the recovery of an empire that had once belonged to the English and that they were simply taking back. "The tale of the lands and seas to which she can lay claim is based both on the dominions mythically reported to have been held by the British King Arthur," writes Yates, "and on those over which the Saxon King Edgar ruled" (Yates, 1975, p. 48). Dee was not the only one to present the acquisition of an empire in these eschatological terms. In his *Book of Prophecies*, Christopher Columbus gives a similar religious justification for Spanish imperialism, arguing that it is part of a four-step sequence

## Prologue: Merlin's Legacy

that will result in the return of Christ. "These were the Christianization of the planet, the discovery of the physical Garden of Eden, a final Crusade to recover Jerusalem from Islam, and, ultimately, the election of a last world emperor to ensure the crushing of Islam, the retaking of the Holy Land, and the return of Christ to the world," writes Louv. "While Columbus had held out for Ferdinand and Isabella to assume this world emperor role, Dee's plan marked a radical departure by suggesting that the world emperor should be Protestant, not Catholic—Elizabeth" (Louv, 2018, p. 138). The legend of Arthur is Dee's crucial supplement to this imperial way of thinking, a historical precedent that reinforces the English claim to an extensive amount of foreign territory:

> Dee argued that during his reign King Arthur had held dominion not only of America, but of thirty countries. If this was indeed the case, then England had at least as much of a spiritual claim to world power as Rome, and all Elizabeth had to do was assume his mantle and become the Arthurian world empress. Even Charles V, the Holy Roman emperor, whose court circle Dee had connections with during his time at Louvain, had long seen Arthur as the model on which the future world ruler would be based. After the Dutch Revolt, it was hoped that Elizabeth would claim Dutch sovereignty—and that she, and not a Habsburg, would become the Arthurian world emperor, uniting the globe under the banner of a reformed Christendom. [...] Maps drawn up by Dee on the foundation of the Arthurian claim to the New World sprawled from Florida to Novaya Zemlya in the Arctic Ocean. Save the Arthurian angle, this was not a new idea—the hope for a last world emperor had long been part of Catholic eschatology [Louv, 2018, p. 137].

This vision of a vast empire, founded on the superiority of British sea power, was a genuine innovation. Indeed, David Armitage argues in *The Ideological Origins of the British Empire* (2000) that "Dee's conception of the British Empire [...] was anomalous in Elizabeth's reign, and entirely at odds with the otherwise consistently maintained Tudor commitment to the freedom of the seas" (Armitage, 2004, p. 107). As such, this heterogeneous assortment of religious and mythological precursors comes together in the hands of Dee to lay the foundations of the British Empire, an imperial madness born out of the tradition of English magic. Just as Merlin places Arthur on the throne, bringing glory, honor, and, most importantly, Christianity to the English nation, so too Dee regards himself as replicating this earlier dynamic with Elizabeth.

## Prologue: Merlin's Legacy

It is crucial, then, to understand *Jonathan Strange and Mr. Norrell* as a novel that emerges from this cultural context, a narrative that functions simultaneously as a product of this historical thread, while also containing an implicit critique of it. Clarke's decision to locate the return of English magic in the milieu and aftermath of the Napoleonic Wars is a timely reminder not only of England's imperial ambitions, but also that this event is part of a recurrent chain of political logic, the roots of which stretch back into a murky past in which history and mythology are inextricably tangled together. What this English national mythology reveals is the extent to which the past can be reshaped and rewritten to transform the present (or indeed, the future) into a self-fulfilling prophecy. This is the "magic" of the writer, the historian, the politician: if a precedent does not exist, then one can be conjured up. The unhappy truth of English magic is the secret of its collaboration with this imperial madness, a sham heroism that masquerades as the epitome of integrity and virtue while leaving behind a trail of injustice and exploitation in its wake. For what kind of king does Strange, the modern Merlin, serve, after all? An impotent madman in George III, whose empire, with the loss of America, appears to be unraveling at the seams. This underlying decadence is the true legacy of Merlin, one that combines England's magical delusions of grandeur with a recurrent refusal to face up to the madness of its imperial sins, a shameful history that Clarke's novel asks her readers to reconsider.

# Chapter 1

# The Fantasy of a Return

## *The Modern Fantasy of Return*

Central to the plot of *Jonathan Strange and Mr. Norrell* is the idea that the practice of English magic, which had once been prevalent in England, slowly disappeared over time. As such, until the emergence of Norrell as England's first modern practical magician, magic in the nineteenth century could only be considered at a distance by historians and theoretical magicians. Clarke thus traces the deterioration of magic from the glory days of the Aureate (Golden Age) magicians, a period that includes Ralph Stokesey, Thomas Godbless, Catherine of Winchester, and of course, the Raven King. The Argentine (Silver Age) magicians that followed in their footsteps, such as Jacques Belasis, Nicholas Goubert, Thomas Lanchester, and Gregory Absalom, all lived during the sixteenth century. These names and figures are, without exception, fictional, but the novel's narrative arc echoes a powerful cultural narrative, which tells how the rise of experimental science and the rationality of Enlightenment philosophy displaced magic and religious superstition. In addition, Clarke replicates a familiar romantic counter-narrative in which magic, after a period of exile, makes a triumphant and heroic return to England's shores.

Beginning with its founding texts, this pattern, in which the poetic idea of restoration follows a period of upheaval and instability, is one of the most common plot devices of the fantasy genre. The eternal winter that plagues Narnia in *The Lion, the Witch and the Wardrobe* (1950), for instance, together with the redemptive spring brought about by Aslan's triumph, establishes a symbolic cycle of infidelity and restitution that draws from "a magic deeper still" than the White Witch's "Deep Magic," an enchantment that reaches "into the stillness and the darkness before Time dawned" (Lewis, 2010, p. 150). As they grow up, the juvenile heroes of Lewis's tales forget their lives and adventures in Narnia, instituting a further sequence of forgetting and rediscovery that begins with *Prince Caspian: The Return to Narnia* (1951) and is repeated throughout the series. The mythology of Middle Earth, by contrast, traces a temporal path of inexorable decline that is quite different from Lewis's. Nonetheless, Tolkien's *The Lord of the Rings* (1954–55) also engages themes of loss and restoration, exemplified by Aragorn's sword, Andúril, which is forged from the fragments of the broken blade of his ancestor, Isildur (Tolkien, 2002, pp. 276–277). Despite their manifest differences, in both of these influential works of fantasy there exists a founding magic, an enchanted origin from which power flows, and to which the narrative must return in order to re-establish its rightful sovereignty over the world.

The crucial aspect of this founding magic is that it derives from a qualitatively different time, a heroic period that predates the setting of the main story. This temporal otherness is central to the appeal of the fantasy of return, for it removes the characters from the reality of the present moment and inserts them into an imagined past—a past that, precisely because it is imagined, is inherently mythological. *Jonathan Strange and Mr. Norrell* reproduces this pattern, but in a way that invites a misreading based on the reader's expectations. Indeed, as Birns points out, the mistaken idea that Clarke's novel portrays a nostalgic and benign return of the "sovereignty" of magic is one of the most common misconceptions about this book:

> The presence of magic does not augur magical sovereignty. By "sovereignty," I mean the tendency to see the irruption of magic onto a realistic world as involving a repeal or regression of modernity. Despite appearing, in its rhetoric of the revival of magic and its fusty, mock-scholarly footnotes, to play into such formulation, Clarke's novel actually sketches its own version of a heterogeneous modernity [Birns, 2020, p. 125].

Imagine how different Lewis's books would be if the Pevensie children walked through the wardrobe only to discover an industrial Narnia that resembled twentieth-century England, with its factories and railways and war machines, but in which the animals had the magical ability to talk. In *Jonathan Strange and Mr. Norrell,* Clarke thus ushers the reader into a world where magic is returning, yet where England is also engaged in a bloody conflict with Napoleon, the slave trade is still

## Chapter 1. The Fantasy of a Return

legal, the British Empire is undertaking a systematic rape of its colonies, and King George III has gone mad, a prisoner in his own castle. "Clarke is looking to the early nineteenth century as the earliest possible modernity," explains Birns, "a time in which magic is intertwined with the world much as it would be today if magic arose now" (Birns, 2020, p. 125). Clarke succeeds in this maneuver because she skillfully adopts the style and mannerisms of an era that, despite its obvious modernity, has already taken on an air of mythological otherness for most contemporary readers. The nineteenth-century fantasies of aristocratic refinement and artistic achievement, epitomized by the twin romantic figures of Austen and Byron, help to eclipse the brutal realities of this period of English history. Clarke's pastiche of the nineteenth century in *Jonathan Strange and Mr. Norrell* thus operates in a double manner, distant enough in time to seem alien from the culture of today, yet grounded in a historical period that, for all its apparent differences, was crucial in influencing the parameters of modern English society. The return of English magic, so familiar at first, is made uncanny by Clarke's willingness to confront the darker side of history.

The impulse to escape from the present is a subjective response to a modern society built around an affirmation of reason as the sole cornerstone of existence. That is the influential argument Max Weber makes in *The Protestant Ethic and the Spirit of Capitalism* (1905), in which he famously describes the growing rationalization of everyday life as an "iron cage" (Weber, 2001, p. 123). In this context, magic's association with the irrational transforms it into an alluring alternative to the disenchanted sphere of a rationally ordered life. The modern human thus resembles Tolkien's character Gollum when it comes to the power and limitations of rational thought: "He hated it and loved it, as he hated and loved himself," Gandalf explains to Frodo (Tolkien, 2002, p. 55). The argument that the ongoing allure of magic is a response to the constraints of modern life is popular among contemporary scholars of magic. In his book *The Place of Enchantment* (2004), for instance, Alex Owen examines the revival of interest in magic in England in the period from 1880 to 1914. Pushing back against the assumption that magic is something that inherently belongs to an earlier, more irrational society, Owen tries to understand "why, in this quintessentially 'modern' moment, late-Victorian and Edwardian women and men became absorbed by metaphysical quests, heterodox spiritual encounters, and occult experimentation, each of which seems to signal the desire for unorthodox numinous experience in a post–Darwinian age" (Owen, 2004, p. 7). The widespread fascination with magic, spiritualism, and theosophy in this period, argues Owen, ought not to be interpreted as a rejection of modernity, but as a response to its limitations.

Examining the magician's place in the cultural imagination, Randall Styers contends that "this figure is configured as quintessentially exotic and alien, a transgressive 'Other' contrasting with the stable modern subject" (Styers, 2004, p. 168). The cultural location of the magician as an outsider, an exceptional subject who refuses to conform to the norms of society, enables them to perform a valuable critique of the limitations of today's society. "Turning the fundamental logic of modernity against itself, various social critics and activists have formulated magic as a line of subversive flight," writes Styers. "Despite so much theorizing about magic—so many attempts to contain and circumscribe it—magic maintains remarkable potency as the 'unthought' of modernity" (Styers, 2004, pp. 169–170). In particular, he argues, magic provides a crucial response to the more utilitarian aspects of modern life:

> The political potency of modern magic as an "anti-culture" has depended on the underlying logic of the cultural and scholarly paradigm stigmatizing magic as nonmodern and condemning it to the margins. The effort to valorize magical practices as subversive of the norms of modernity adopts the logical structure of this paradigm but then turns the paradigm against itself. This move has been important to various countercultural groups that have adopted magic as a trope for social critique. [...] Magic holds out a promise of escape from the cold instrumentalism of modernity [Styers, 2004, p. 214].

Styers's analysis makes fascinating reading in the context of Norrell's attempts to reform the social position of magic, for in *Jonathan Strange and Mr. Norrell* magic is a lowly, even debased occupation: "A gentleman could not do magic. Magic was what street sorcerers pretended to do in order to rob children of their pennies. [...] It had low connexions. [...] A gentleman might study the history of magic (nothing could be nobler) but he could not do any" (Clarke, 2015, pp. 4–5). Norrell's efforts to make the practice of magic respectable are the opposite of Styers's description of the typical "outsider" position of the magician. It is thus left to Strange—a gentleman *and* an outsider—to reclaim the critical role that Styers assigns to the figure of the magician.

## Chapter 1. The Fantasy of a Return

In his book *The Myth of Disenchantment* (2017), Jason Josephson-Storm provides a powerful alternative to this Weberian strand of interpretation. Central to Josephson-Storm's critique is a sweeping examination of the trope of the "return" in cultural narratives about modernity. Starting with a dramatic reassessment of the historical importance of terms like "science" and "the Enlightenment," Josephson-Storm launches into a genealogy of the logic of "return" that begins with the German romantics of the late eighteenth and early nineteenth centuries. Their interest in the mythology of earlier times, he argues, possesses a quality that goes beyond mere nostalgia. The romantic fascination with the mythologies of bygone eras springs less from a longing to return to ancient ways, than the distressing feeling among these moderns that they themselves had no mythology of their own. As such, they regarded the myths of the ancients not only with admiration, but also a new yearning for a cultural dimension they felt had been lost:

> [T]he real myth was not [...] Orientalized reconstructions of Aryan mythology nor Teutonic revivals. Its core was the very idea that, as Schlegel stated, "we have no mythology." In a nutshell, the myth born from this philosophical conjuncture was an anti-myth, a myth that described itself in terms of longing, absence, and mythlessness. Its paradox is that only by being a myth that there was no myth could its status as myth go unnoticed and hence not be demystified. It was a myth in search of myth. Insofar as this myth is still our myth—or at least an animating narrative across many sectors of modern society—their project worked [Josephson-Storm, 2017, p. 64].

The example of the German romantics, argues Josephson-Storm, created the basic template for modern thought, a formula repeated "so often that it can sound like a fable" (Josephson-Storm, 2017, p. 65). In its triumphant mode, this paradigm begins and ends with the tale of how "at a particular moment the darkness of superstition, myth, or religion began to give way to modern light, exchanging traditional unreason for technology and rationality" (Josephson-Storm, 2017, p. 65). When told from a romantic, melancholic perspective, by contrast, "it can sound like the inauguration of our tragic alienation from an idealized past" (Josephson-Storm, 2017, p. 65). Josephson-Storm argues that this logic has been used to rewrite how we interpret not only the recent past, but also other time periods—the ancient Greeks, for instance, have been the focus of particular attention by modern thinkers from this disenchanted perspective.

Its influence can similarly be felt in the "return" of English magic in *Jonathan Strange and Mr. Norrell*, which appeals to modern readers precisely because the prevalence of the Weberian narrative of disenchantment instills the sense that, in losing magic, we have lost a connection to our historical roots as human beings. In *Religion and the Decline of Magic* (1973), Keith Thomas argues that this attitude stands in stark contrast to the attitudes of the people actually living when magic was prevalent, who typically feared and avoided its disruptive power. The medieval scholar Roger Bacon, for instance, was "much besmirched by the assumption that mathematics was part of the black art," reports Thomas, "and it was notorious that the Edwardian reformers had destroyed mathematical manuscripts at Oxford under the delusion that they were conjuring books" (Thomas, 2003, p. 430). Clarke self-consciously appropriates this yearning for a return of magic to modern England through the establishment of the "Norrelite" position, which seeks to suppress the role of unreason in the production of magic, thus detaching it from its historical connections to Faerie and the Raven King. The "Strangeite" position that opposes it represents a romantic backlash to this dynamic, inspiring Strange's journey into the heart of irrationality and madness.

This mindset does not originally derive from English culture, Josephson-Storm argues, but emerges from an identifiably German romantic rethinking of Spinozist pantheism. Despite the outward piety of Spinoza's language, the German romantics rightly identified an incipient atheism in his philosophical system: "It was not physics that produced the nihilistic clockwork universe, but philosophy" (Josephson-Storm, 2017, p. 74). This turn is particularly noticeable in German discussions of the death of God, a concept articulated in the 1830s and 1840s by Heinrich Heine, Bruno Bauer, and Max Stirner, well before its more famous pronouncement by Nietzsche's madman in *The Gay Science* (1882). "Taken together, these scattered references to the death of God are still not sociological descriptions of secularization, nor are they sober reflections on de-Christianization," argues Josephson-Storm, "rather, they are modern jeremiads or laments. They indicate more a presence of grief than an absence of religion" (Josephson-Storm, 2017, p. 75). The legacy of the German romantics

## Chapter 1. The Fantasy of a Return

resonates in the growing ambivalence of nineteenth-century thought about religion, caught as it is in the disjunction between atheistic rationality and spiritual longing.

A crucial text for this unfolding discourse is a poem by Friedrich Schiller titled "The Gods of Greece" (1788), the impact of which Josephson-Storm traces in *The Myth of Disenchantment*. The real target of Schiller's poetic lament lies in the poet's opposition to the reduction of the world to pure mechanism. "Schiller's hostility to mechanism was not an advocacy for faith or a repudiation of reason," writes Josephson-Storm. "Rather, he wanted to reject a clockwork cosmos in favor of a living world" (Josephson-Storm, 2017, p. 83). The influence of Schiller's poem has been crucial to the creation of the paradigm of a romantic "return" that, for all its outward longing for a return to an earlier time, nonetheless springs from an entirely modern impulse:

> Taken together, these early responses suggested a lost animist or pagan past in which humanity was in harmony with nature, and they often share an attempt to pinpoint the moment that this bond was shattered. [...] "The Gods of Greece" is a melancholy elegy for a lost golden age. Schiller's 1789 lectures on universal history, however, are more hopeful. [...] For Schiller, paradise lost could not only be regained, but perhaps even improved. This idea of progress as return in a greater synthesis was not unique to Schiller. It is an example of what M.H. Abrams calls the "Romantic Spiral," the historiographical structure that fuses narratives of historical decline and progress to suggest that the goal of history is a return of the past in a higher key [Josephson-Storm, 2017, pp. 85–86].

The yearning for a return of a magical world cannot be truly subversive, argues Josephson-Storm, because it is a symptom of disenchantment, so that for all its apparent negativity it actually plays a vital role in the maintenance of that system. The fantasy of a return is problematic because the thing supposedly being returned to is only a fiction of the past, a colonized reinterpretation of history that is really a disavowed modernity in antique clothing. Modernity thus claims disingenuously to long for the return of enchantment, but in truth is only willing to accept it on the contradictory terms of a secular disenchantment that makes such a return impossible. In much the same way, Norrell aims to restore the practice of English magic, but only on terms that are rational and respectable, in a manner that suppresses and ignores the historical logic of unreason that is magic's true foundation. Nothing would be more terrifying to Norrell than the true return of English magic in the form of the Raven King, which is precisely why this eventuality is unleashed in the final stages of Clarke's novel.

## *The Englishness of English Magic*

Equally problematic in *Jonathan Strange and Mr. Norrell* is the return of a specifically *English* form of magic. The very notion of the "Englishness" of magic, after all, is far from being an easily definable, stable entity. Ronald Hutton's *The Pagan Religions of the Ancient British Isles* (1991), a study of the early forms of religious belief in Great Britain, helped raise awareness of a historical record that has, in turn, inspired its own fantasy of a return through popular neo-pagan revivals such as Wicca and Druidism. "The magical quest is [...] a philosophical quest for the truth, and yet the story of magic is one of endless fantasies, fibs and fictions," write Philip Carr-Gomm and Richard Heygate in *The Book of English Magic* (2010). "Much of the recounted history, certainly before the end of the twentieth century, of Druids, witches, Freemasons, alchemists and Rosicrucians is simply not true. Sometimes this is the result of deliberate deception, sometimes of poor scholarship combined with wishful thinking" (Carr-Gomm & Heygate, 2010, p. 388). The more deeply one looks into the genealogy of English magic, the more questions arise about just how "English" English magic really is.

Clarke's novel probes the mythology of what it means to be English by revealing its contradictions to the careful reader. In the wake of England's victory in the Napoleonic Wars, for example, she reflects on how Lord Wellington is celebrated as the epitome of the English character. "Every schoolboy impersonates Wellington at least once a week, and so do his younger sisters," Clarke writes. "Wellington embodies every English virtue. He is Englishness carried to perfection. If the French carry Napoleon in their bellies (which apparently they do), then we carry Wellington in our hearts" (Clarke, 2015, p. 373). This outburst of national devotion is immediately undercut by a footnote in which Clarke observes sardonically: "Of course it may be objected that Wellington himself was *Irish*, but a patriotic English pen does not stoop to answer such quibbling" (Clarke, 2015, p. 373). Another telling example occurs in Chapter 54 of *Jonathan Strange and Mr. Norrell*, in which

## Chapter 1. The Fantasy of a Return

Strange and Miss Greysteel partake in the following exchange about Lord Byron:

> Miss Greysteel asked him about Lord Byron.
> "Oh!" said Strange. "He does not intend to return to England. He can write poems anywhere. Whereas in my own case, English magic was shaped by England—just as England herself was shaped by magic. The two go together. You cannot separate them."
> "You mean," said Miss Greysteel, frowning a little, "that English minds and history and so forth were shaped by magic. You are speaking metaphorically."
> "No, I was speaking quite literally" [Clarke, 2015, p. 784].

If an English poet like Byron leaves England, the impression of the land on his character is so profoundly formative that, even after his departure to other countries, the poetry he writes remains, in a sense, English. In the same way, an English magician who leaves England may likewise be said to continue practicing English magic, as Strange proves during his sojourn in Venice.

In a 2007 interview with Martyn Drake, Clarke provides a more detailed explanation of this connection. "Is English magic very different from that of other places?" queries Drake. "Did other nations lose their magic as England did, and if so, is it coming back? Can you do English magic if you aren't in England, or is it tied to the land?" (Clarke, 2007a) Clarke replies:

> Yes, you can do English magic if you aren't in England. We know this because Strange does magic in Portugal, Spain, Italy and Belgium (and for an hour or so in America). Nevertheless English magic is tied to the land. [...] English magicians developed magic—made it less fundamental, less natural, but ultimately they were drawing on the goodwill of the English Wind, the English Rain, the English Hills and those Stars that you can see from the Sussex Wolds or Birmingham or Carlisle. So English magic was like a conversation between the magicians and England [Clarke, 2007a].

There is a political subtext to Drake's questions, since to affirm the idea that there exists an inherent tie between English magic and English soil would be to echo the kind of jingoistic nationalism that became prominent in the post–Napoleonic era. While Clarke characterizes English magic as "a conversation between the magicians and England" (Clarke,

2007a), her observation carefully avoids specifying that those magicians must actually be English for that connection to be made. Indeed, later in the same response, Clarke makes some important qualifications to her initial answer:

> On the other hand, how English is English magic? As we've seen it comes from fairies. And John Uskglass didn't think of himself as English—not at first anyway. He claimed to be Norman, which (if it were true) meant that his grandfather would have come over from Normandy with William the Conqueror. And in the 19th century Jonathan Strange's mother was Scottish [Clarke, 2007a].

There is thus a double movement in Clarke's definition of English magic, a sleight of hand that affirms its particular connection to the English landscape and its elements, while at the same time destabilizing the Englishness of English magic. So while Strange and Norrell are both Englishmen, Strange's mother is Scottish, the fairies are from another world, and the Raven King, the ultimate practitioner of English magic, is reputedly from a Norman family.

The latter example is particularly important because the Raven King is so forcefully associated with the history and power of English magic. In Strange's scathing review of Lord Portishead's Norrellite tract *Essay on the Extraordinary Revival of English Magic, &c.*, for instance, he points to the glaring paradox that underpins Norrell's concept of modern English magic: it self-consciously excludes and suppresses the importance of the Raven King, even though without him English magic would not exist (Clarke, 2015, p. 532). It was the Raven King, Strange argues, who set down the most basic terms of English magic, a tradition from which it cannot reasonably be detached:

> English Magic is the strange house we magicians inhabit. It is built upon foundations that JOHN USKGLASS made and we ignore those foundations at our peril. They should be studied and their nature understood so that we can learn what they will support and what they will not. Otherwise cracks will appear, letting in winds from God-knows-where. The corridors will lead us to places we never intended to go [Clarke, 2015, p. 531].

This gesture by Strange is an excellent example of the first movement in the sleight of hand identified above. It establishes the Raven King as the embodiment of English magic, the builder of its most

## Chapter 1. The Fantasy of a Return

crucial "foundations," while carefully ignoring the vexed question of the Englishness of John Uskglass.

The glimpses the reader is given into the Raven King's history confirm that his Englishness is not an easy thing to establish. Being a king in Faerie certainly does not disqualify him—one may, after all, still be an English king in Faerie, in the same way that Lord Byron continues to be an English poet in Switzerland, and Strange an English magician in Venice. The Raven King's reputed Norman origins, however, mark a destabilization of his English identity, for the first few monarchs after the Norman Conquest, beginning with William the Conqueror, did not regard themselves as English. The Norman language they spoke, as well as their attachments to large estates on the European continent, especially in France, did little to encourage their identification with England. The Norman lords living in England after the Conquest ruled over an Anglo-Saxon population from which they were similarly alienated by language and culture. When Childermass meets the Raven King late in the novel, he can hear a conglomeration of cultural influences in the latter's accent: the northern English accent predominates in the Raven King's speech, but Childermass can also hear hints of a Scandinavian heritage, overlaid by a strong French tinge that derives from John Uskglass's Norman background (Clarke, 2015, p. 970). Childermass's sensitivity to the Raven King's northern accent reflects, of course, his own background as a Yorkshireman. It is also an allusion to the division of England into north and south, a fictional partition that is referenced several times in *Jonathan Strange and Mr. Norrell* without being clarified or explained. As such, the historical monarchs are referred to in Clarke's novel as the Kings of Southern England, with John Uskglass ruling during this period as the King of the North; by the time of Strange and Norrell, the two kingdoms have been united into a single England. To which of these divisions, north or south, does English magic properly belong? References are occasionally made to magical traditions that tie the north to John Uskglass—there is, for example, the prevailing custom that buildings which have fallen into ruin are the property of the Raven King (Clarke, 2015, p. 268)—but English magic seems to work just as well at the country's southern borders, as evidenced by the protective spells that Norrell sets up to repel the French. Clarke's alternative history of England is left provocatively obscure, a country unified despite having been, at the peak of its magical history, divided into two parts.

## English Magic and Imperial Madness

The Raven King's claim to Englishness is further brought into question by his implicit ties to Wales. No Welsh connection is alluded to directly in the text of *Jonathan Strange and Mr. Norrell*, yet it is hinted at repeatedly through the mythical echoes that Clarke builds into her story. Consider the appellation "John Uskglass," for instance, which the reader is told is probably not the Raven King's true name, but instead belonged to a Norman lord who died in 1097. While the Raven King subsequently declared Uskglass to be his father, the connection remains apocryphal, so that the two men may not have been related at all (Clarke, 2015, p. 957). Uskglass is not a Norman name, not even in its modified French form of d'Uskglass, but instead is of Welsh origin. The word "Usk," in particular, points toward Wales, where both a castle and a river bear this title, each of which has connections to Arthurian legend. Yet it is not Usk Castle that provides the strongest connection to the Raven King, but another ancient ruin known as Dinas Brân. This structure predates the Norman invasion, and is named after the legendary Welsh king Bran the Blessed, whose name means "raven":

> Dinas Brân is the most likely site of the Grail castle in Britain. In medieval literature it was known as Corbenic, a derivation of the name raven or crow. Bran, whose name also means raven, possessed a life-restoring cauldron, one of the prototypes of the Holy Grail. He is often associated with Bron, the Fisher King[.] [...] Bran's head, which provided nourishment like a Grail, was eventually buried at the Tower of London until exhumed by Arthur. His ravens there continue to guard the land [Begg & Begg, 2008, p. 3].

The metamorphosis of this legend is given a further twist by a passage from *Don Quixote* (1605–15), in which Quixote relates how King Arthur, "according to an ancient tradition divulged throughout that kingdom of Great Britain, did not die but was, by sorcerer's art, turned into a raven, and who, in due course, will recover his sceptre and kingdom, and reign again; for which reason no Englishman has ever been known from that day to this to kill a raven?" (Cervantes, 2000, p. 96). In his essay "Cornwall and the Matter of Britain" (2019), Oliver J. Padel briefly traces the historical influence of this permutation of the Arthurian myth, showing how it began in the early twelfth century and persisted well into the nineteenth (Padel, 2019, p. 268). There are thus many echoes in *Jonathan Strange and Mr. Norrell* that link John Uskglass to Welsh mythology, not English.

## Chapter 1. The Fantasy of a Return

The Englishness of English magic is further brought into question if we look beyond the borders of Great Britain to examine English magic from a more global perspective. Apart from the realm of Faerie, there is little acknowledgment in *Jonathan Strange and Mr. Norrell* of the rich tradition of magic from the European continent and beyond that has had such a profound influence on the historical development of English magic. Yet scholars of magic repeatedly emphasize that magic in England has always been permeated by a range of outside inspirations, which it has then integrated into its practices and ideas:

> [I]t developed as a result of a continuous stream of influences from abroad, which included those of Nordic culture from the ninth century, alchemical ideas from Arabia in the thirteenth century, NeoPlatonic theories from Italy in the fifteenth century, Rosicrucian mysticism from Germany in the seventeenth century, and a cluster of influences from France during its nineteenth-century occult revival. The most powerful influence of all came from the Jewish mysticism of the kabbalah, which reached the world of "high magic" in England in the sixteenth century. By the late nineteenth century it had become central to the majority of ceremonial magic being practised in the country [Carr-Gomm & Heygate, 2010, p. 331].

While these influences refer to the practice of academic magic (or "high magic") in England, Carr-Gomm and Heygate note that this phenomenon also extends, albeit to a lesser extent, to the local magic (or "low magic") practiced in villages and provincial areas. "Romany (Gypsy) traditions have also been a continuous feature in England since the sixteenth century," they point out, "but have been less influential, due to a lack of written texts, and remained confined to the world of 'low magic': of fortune-telling, charming and herbal healing" (Carr-Gomm & Heygate, 2010, p. 331). There is no aspect of English magic, therefore, that can claim to be a "purely" English magic. English magic has always been a patchwork of ideas and practices transplanted from elsewhere and adapted to local conditions.

A glance at the magical tradition in the wider European context reveals a similar pattern. The extensive suspicion shown toward magic derives from misgivings about its often-secretive nature, on the one hand, and the sense that it belongs to a foreign culture, on the other. "One reason for this scorn of magic was an exoticism ascribed to it as early as Heraclitus (fl. c. 500 BCE)," writes Simon During. "The Greeks believed that their thought was based on imported concepts, and of the foreign ideas so absorbed, magic was pre-eminent. It was associated with the ancient Eastern and Egyptian peoples, especially with the Persian Magi (whence 'magic' itself), and often with one man, Zoroaster (fl. sixth century BCE)" (During, 2002, p. 5). In *Magic and Superstition in Europe* (2007), Michael D. Bailey observes how the Greco-Roman suspicion of magic's association with Persian and Egyptian cults in turn affected Christianity's early struggles for legitimacy:

> Roman authors such as Tacitus (ca. 55–117) and Suetonius (ca. 69–140) derided Christian practices as superstitions. [...] [T]he figure of Christ himself presented problems. Christians recognized him as a god—indeed, as God—invoked him in their rites, and claimed to wield power in his name. Yet Christians also maintained that Christ was human. To the casual observer in antiquity, then, here was a man, an itinerant beggar, who claimed considerable prophetic, healing, and other powers, and who worked wonders to attract a following. This was the very image of the *magos*. The charge that Christ was in fact a magician troubled Christianity for several hundred years [Bailey, 2007, pp. 48–49].

As Christianity gained political and cultural ascendancy, it was able to bend this logic to its own purposes. A key part of its strategy was to overcode indigenous local practices with those of the church. "Much energy was spent in demonstrating that holy water was the Roman *aqua lustralis*, that wakes were the *Bacchanalia*, Shrove Tuesday celebrations *Saturnalia*, Rogation processions *ambarvalia*, and so forth," explains Thomas (Thomas, 2003, pp. 74–75). Indeed, argues Wouter J. Hanegraaff, the "notions of secrecy and concealment" that are so important to the occult tradition helped "its Christian adherents," who "always needed to make the argument that beneath the surface crust of pagan religion there lay a hidden core of Christian truth" (Hanegraaff, 2012, p. 64). Richard Kieckhefer thus reminds readers in *Magic in the Middle Ages* (2014) that "to understand the overall patterns of medieval magic we must be aware of these borrowings from diverse cultures" (Kieckhefer, 2014, p. 2). Magic in European culture began as "something sinister, something threatening" because "the magi were foreigners with exotic skills that aroused apprehension," observes Kieckhefer, and so this apprehension has repeatedly been "extended to cover the sinister activities of occultists whether foreign or domestic" (Kieckhefer, 2014, p. 10). What this history demonstrates is that English magic simply

## Chapter 1. The Fantasy of a Return

cannot be a pure expression of blood and soil, because its ideas and practices have always been produced from a heterogeneous mix of precursors that originate from outside its borders.

In *Jonathan Strange and Mr. Norrell*, it is the Norrellite conception of English magic that seeks to suppress these influences. Norrell actively attempts to erase the Raven King from the modern idea of magic, a step he takes to distance himself from street magicians like Vinculus and so appeal to the upper echelons of society. A similar logic dictates his general refusal to undertake fairy magic. When he encounters the gentleman with the thistledown hair at Lady Pole's bedside, for instance, Norrell angrily accuses the fairy of wishing to control English magic for perverse ends, turning England into a place fit only for "your degenerate race" (Clarke, 2015, pp. 212–213). Norrell's suppression of foreign influences on English magic is less visible, and expresses itself mainly through his attempts to monopolize the supply of books about magic. When Segundus and Honeyfoot first visit Norrell early in the novel, for instance, they discover a seventeenth-century book on his shelves they have never seen before titled *The Excellences of Christo-Judaic Magick*. Norrell swiftly removes it from their hands, stating that the work is of no importance and decrying the author as "a liar, a drunkard, an adulterer and a rogue. I am glad he has been so completely forgot" (Clarke, 2015, p. 15). With the notable exceptions of Merlin and Valentine Greatrakes, Clarke studiously avoids mentioning any magicians drawn from historical accounts, so the author of *The Excellences of Christo-Judaic Magick* is no doubt a fictionalized version of a real figure, as Owen Davies suggests. "In her bestseller *Jonathan Strange and Mr. Norrell* (2004), Susanna Clarke re-creates an early-nineteenth-century England where learned magic once again becomes a profound force after centuries in the shadows," he observes. "Old magic books are central to her clever, gothic re-imagining of the occult milieu of the period, mentioning titles that sound familiar to the reader but are in fact her own inventions" (Davies, 2009, p. 282). The author of the book that Segundus singles out is thus probably based on Giovanni Pico della Mirandola (1463–1494), famous in the history of magic for introducing the Jewish Kabbalah into occult thought. After the invention of the printing press in the late sixteenth century, the Renaissance saw a widespread cross-pollination of magical ideas that "spread through the medium of print" (Davies, 2009, p. 46). Davies contributes his own critique of the fantasy of a return by pointing out that recent scholarship has tended to see the Renaissance flowering of magic as a continuation, rather than a break, with medieval culture. "There was no 'rebirth' of magic, no great break with the past, but rather a continuation and development of medieval ideas about the secrets encoded in ancient texts, be they pagan, Jewish, Islamic, or Christian" (Davies, 2009, p. 46). We should likewise be wary of the "return" of English magic presented in *Jonathan Strange and Mr. Norrell*, an event that is undermined by the doubtful Englishness of its magic, as well as by an increasing skepticism among historians and scholars that magic ever diminished in the manner described by the Weberian narrative of disenchantment.

## *Magic's Persistence*

The growing skepticism among scholars about this disenchanted narrative of magic's disappearance and return derives, in part, from a greater sensitivity to differences in social class. Paul Kléber Monod argues in *Solomon's Secret Arts: The Occult in the Age of Enlightenment* (2013), for instance, that previous writers on this topic—he criticizes Thomas for this shortcoming, for example—have tended to favor the history of academic magic, practiced mostly by a small group of intellectuals from privileged backgrounds who recorded their ideas using the written word, over the much more extensive practice of low magic among the common people. The latter group was often illiterate, and so their mainly oral tradition has been obscured, as a result, from scholarly histories. Recent scholarship has nonetheless established that, despite the ebbs and flows of academic magic, the common tradition remained strong for a long time. "It is now evident that, in England as in other parts of Europe, ordinary people did not cast off their adherence to magic," writes Monod, "no matter what their social betters might have thought, so that the question of when magic declined has become a much more complicated one" (Monod, 2013, p. 7). It is particularly complicated because, while magic may have lost its status in some higher circles of society, among the lower classes those beliefs remained deeply influential. Magic's persistence represents a particular problem for the narrative of return, for magic can hardly return if it never left in the first place.

## Chapter 1. The Fantasy of a Return

Monod is careful to distinguish this continuity of belief in magic among the common people from recent twentieth-century reformulations of magical practices. "Revisionist assertions such as these are no longer particularly original or controversial, especially in relation to witchcraft," argues Monod. "To assume that magic survived into the modern period has become a new orthodoxy" (Monod, 2013, p. 8). The fashionable modern version of magic that arises in this period is, for Monod, little more than a mixture of clever marketing and wishful thinking that bears little historical scrutiny:

> Under this scrutiny, the agelessness of the occult turns out to be an illusion—or, in many cases, a mystification, because its adherents have made such efforts to disguise its recent origins. It seems doubtful that much in the commercialized occultism of today can be traced back beyond the late nineteenth century. [...] Even the foundations of serious occult thinking owe more to modern anxieties, and to modern marketing techniques, than to the builders of pyramids or ziggurats. [...] [T]he occult as we know it today seems largely to be an "invented tradition." Its direct evocation of the past, its venerable heritage and alleged roots in "the wisdom of the ages," have as often as not been misappropriated, distorted, embellished or even fabricated, whether out of enthusiasm, ignorance or just plain chicanery [Monod, 2013, p. 2].

With Monod's warning in mind, therefore, let us consider the truth of magic's persistence by examining the recent scholarship about the ongoing belief in magic and fairies among the English lower classes, a continuance that has too often been overlooked in the historical narrative.

One of the key figures engaged in this kind of revision is Owen Davies, who has written extensively about witchcraft and magic in England in studies like *Popular Magic: Cunning-Folk in English History* (2003), the title of which reflects its focus on the magic practices of the common people. In this book, Davies draws the reader's attention to the important cultural role played for many centuries by the so-called "cunning-folk" in English society. "The term cunning-folk is little known today," observes Davies. "Yet a century ago everyone in rural society would have been familiar with the term, and two hundred years ago the majority of the population, in both town and country, would have known of at least one cunning-man or cunning-woman" (Davies, 2003, p. vii). Consider, for instance, the pivotal role played by Conjuror

Trendle in Thomas Hardy's 1888 short story "The Withered Arm." Roger Ebbatson points out how the cunning-man's role in Hardy's tale is connected to the outlook of its protagonist, the milk-maid Rhoda:

> The belief system in which Rhoda is embedded demands an extreme sensitivity to all kinds of social conduct, and to every manifestation of the natural world. The common denominators of her culture are orality and the natural rhythm of the seasons, and it is these factors which come into play in the recommendation to her lucklessly pretty rival, Gertrude Lodge, to seek the advice of the white wizard, Conjuror Trundle, in the recesses of Egdon Heath [Ebbatson, 1993, p. 132].

"The Withered Arm" supports Davies's point about the important social role that continued to be played by the cunning-folk well into the nineteenth century. These men and women, he argues, were "a professional type that for centuries was as integral to English life as the clergyman, constable and doctor" (Davies, 2003, p. vii). As such, their role is central to the persistence of magic among the common people.

Another important contribution to the scholarly discussion of cunning-folk is Emma Wilby's *Cunning Folk and Familiar Spirits: Shamanistic Visionary Traditions in Early Modern British Witchcraft and Magic* (2005), which reiterates the way that such figures have typically been excluded from the history of magic. Wilby emphasizes the enchanted nature of the world that early modern people inhabited. "Powerful occult forces permeated life at every level," she writes. "From the moment of birth, the early modern poor were immersed in this magical universe and [...] it was their beliefs and rituals which enabled them to deal with the invisible web of supernatural forces which lay behind it" (Wilby, 2005, pp. 8–10). Wilby also points out that the influence of Christian ideas is far less important than is usually supposed. Many common people did not attend church at all, and what religious knowledge they did have was often mingled with ancient folk beliefs. "The early modern 'fairy faith' [...] was an amalgamation of many of the animistic beliefs and rituals surrounding nature spirits, deities, ghosts and so on which had not been completely homogenized into Catholic hagiolatry and the cult of the dead" (Wilby, 2005, p. 17). One of the key differences that separates Wilby from her predecessors is her focus on what she calls the "shamanistic" aspects of English magic, which include the use of animal familiars, spirits, demons, and, of course, fairies:

## Chapter 1. The Fantasy of a Return

> If the familiar spirits used by witches have received little attention from historians, those used by cunning folk have received even less. [...] Keith Thomas seldom mentions the use of familiar spirits by cunning folk [...] [and implies] that the role of spirits in the magical practice of cunning folk was minimal. No historians have subsequently contradicted Thomas's assertions and the cunning man or woman's familiar is largely absent from academic studies of early modern British magic and witchcraft. Owen Davies's recent work on English cunning folk maintains Thomas's emphasis. Despite acknowledging that "learned conjurors with their grimoires commanded demons, spirits and angels to come to their aid, [while] the more humble could, instead, call upon the services of the fairies," Davies only touches briefly on popular fairy-conjuring activities [Wilby, 2005, p. 51].

Wilby's revelations about the importance of shamanistic practices to English magic reiterates how Norrell's distaste for fairy magic is not a recent phenomenon, that even among historians this crucial element has been obscured or even erased from the record. This effacement, in turn, reflects a class prejudice that accords with Norrell's attempts to make magic respectable by removing it from its common, folk origins and giving it an exclusively academic foundation.

In *Romanticism and Popular Magic: Poetry and Cultures of the Occult in the 1790s* (2019), Stephanie Elizabeth Churms similarly explores how magic, far from disappearing in the wake of Enlightenment rationality, remained a persistent and vital practice in everyday English life. One of the key reasons why magic became less visible during the 1790s, she argues, has to do with a crucial change in English politics after the French Revolution. "After the war with France began in 1793, any culture that ran counter to orthodox systems of belief would be regarded with suspicion" (Churms, 2019, p. 83), with particular mistrust directed toward secret societies with magical associations—"Freemasons, Rosicrucians, Mesmerists, Swedenborgians, Avignon Prophets, to name but a few of those accused of participating in this radical intellectual climate of occult subversion" (Churms, 2019, p. 84). So it was that politics at the turn of the nineteenth century demanded a drastic redefinition of English patriotism in terms that created a negative association between magic, radical politics, and irrationality. Churms thus provides some revelatory readings of texts by Wordsworth, Coleridge, and Southey, demonstrating the extent to which these romantic poets inhabit a world where magic is a living, breathing tradition.

## English Magic and Imperial Madness

Recent scholarship on magic in England thus complicates the disenchantment narrative of disappearance and return by showing that a living culture of magic persisted in England well into modern times. For all their apparent opposition, Strange and Norrell represent the opposing sides of a peculiar form of disenchanted chauvinism, epitomized by Strange's remarks about the return of the Raven King.

> Though we bewail the end of English magic and say it is long gone from us and inquire of each other how it was possible that we came to lose something so precious, let us not forget that it also waits for us at England's end and one day we will no more be able to escape the Raven King than, in this present Age, we can bring him back [Clarke, 2015, p. 268].

Clarke presents a powerful alternative to this perspective in "The Ladies of Grace Adieu," a short story that eschews entirely this grandiose, teleological narrative. The three cunning-women in the title story provide a crucial juxtaposition to Strange, who is told by Cassandra that "for all your cleverness, [you] are at war, even with yourself," whereas the three female magicians are "as free [...] as any women in the kingdom" (Clarke, 2007b, pp. 34–35). In "The Ladies of Grace Adieu," Clarke shows her readers a magical practice that has never been held captive by a timeline of disappearance and return, but simply exists as a timeless, ingrained potential, an immanence that flows out of the trees and rivers of England, lurking like an owl in the dark.

## Chapter 2

# Writing, Text, Mythology

## *All the Texts of the World*

Near the conclusion of *Jonathan Strange and Mr. Norrell*, Stephen Black is granted the power to wreak destruction on the enemy who has stolen his peace of mind, the malevolent fairy known only as the gentleman with the thistle-down hair. This sudden power is granted through a spell cast by Strange, who addresses his magical command to the natural world, the source from which English magic appears to derive:

> "And now for the magic itself," said Strange. He picked up the book and began to recite the spell. He addressed the trees of England; the hills of England; the sunlight, water, birds, earth and stones. He addressed them all, one after the other, and exhorted them to place themselves in the hands of the nameless slave [Clarke, 2015, pp. 980–981].

The presence of magic has a distinctive effect whenever it is deployed in Clarke's novel: it transforms the world into a mysterious kind of writing that the wielder of magic must decipher in order to take hold of its power. That is why, when Strange's spell takes effect, the world around Stephen is dramatically transformed: "Suddenly everything had meaning" (Clarke, 2015, p. 981). Just as Strange had spoken to the trees, the hills, the sunlight, and so on, so too they now turn to Stephen, looking to him for a response. "*The bare branches against the sky were a writing and, though he did not want to, he could read it,*" writes Clarke. "*He saw that it was a question put to him by the trees*" (Clarke, 2015, p. 981). Stephen experiences the magic of the world as a script, a text written in an occult language that he cannot fully understand.

Stephen's experience is not unique: Norrell's servant Childermass detects a similar disturbance in Chapter 46, a magical intrusion that culminates with Lady Pole's assault on his master. While recovering from the wound received in this attack, Childermass exclaims: "The sky spoke to me!" (Clarke, 2015, p. 659). He then points out the implications of his magical experience to Norrell by reminding his master that the Aureate magicians considered the natural world to possess a kind of subjectivity, leading them habitually to interact with trees and rivers in the course of their magical practice (Clarke, 2015, p. 658).* In the mythology of Clarke's fictional universe, the Aureates belong to the golden age of English magic, an era that roughly aligns with the medieval period. They comprise the pre-eminent magicians of the English tradition, including Thomas Godbless, Ralph de Stokesey, Catherine of Winchester, and John Uskglass, the Raven King (Clarke, 2015, p. 529). Norrell, who is determined to transform English magic into a modern, rational, and most important of all, *respectable* discipline, is vehemently opposed to the ideas and practices of the Aureate period. He thus replies to Childermass's inquiry by confirming the historical accuracy of this depiction of the Aureates, who received their ideas about the connection between nature and magic from the fairies who served them, but dismisses the idea that such a mindset is strictly necessary, pointing to the fact that he performs magic that does not rely on these devices (Clarke, 2015, pp. 658–659). Indeed, Norrell's disenchanted form of magic can also make nature speak, transforming rain into battleships and enticing stones to speak their secrets.

The form in which English magic in *Jonathan Strange and Mr. Norrell* is thus repeatedly presented to the reader is that of a text. It is not a human text, however, but a natural one, a system of writing that is inscribed on the hills and trees and rivers of England, a hidden narrative that the magicians of a former age once knew how to decipher and manipulate with ease, but has since been lost. This notion of the world as a text, in turn, has a crucial history outside of Clarke's fictional world. Peter Harrison, for instance, observes that the twelfth century was a turning point for how the order of nature was understood. In *The Territories of Science and Religion* (2015), he explains that medieval scholars thought of the Holy Scriptures and the works of nature as complementary texts that reveal God's message to humanity:

---

*When Piranesi reads about the magical rituals of Laurence Arne-Sayles in his Journals, he notes: "One sentence puzzles me: *The world was constantly speaking to Ancient Man.* I do not understand why this sentence is in the past tense. The World still speaks to me every day" (Clarke, 2020, p. 154). Dwelling in the House has made Piranesi into a natural magician.

## Chapter 2. Writing, Text, Mythology

> [T]he Church Fathers were to speak of two linked modes of divine communication—one in the book of scripture, and one in the book of nature. While the natural world was distinct from God, and hence nondivine, in various ways the creatures were thought to bear mute testimony to their divine origins. In a certain sense, the world was the bearer of the divine image, although, owing to the fallen condition of the cosmos and its human tenants, that image was faint and difficult to discern. But with the guidance provided by scripture the language of the book of nature could be understood. Reading scripture and nature together become an integral part of medieval contemplative practice [Harrison, 2015, p. 56].

This influential notion of reading nature as a divine text can be seen, for instance, in the work of the Swiss physician Paracelsus, who believed that a divine purpose was written, like a signature, on all things. "There is nothing that Nature has not signed in such a way that man may discover its essence" (Paracelsus, 1990, p. 129). These ideas were so powerful that they endured well into the seventeenth century. "Newton and fellow adepts recognized no radical difference between their scientific and textual studies," observes Charles Webster in *From Paracelsus to Newton: Magic and the Making of Modern Science* (1982). "The analogy between the book of nature and the work of revelation was a commonplace" (Webster, 1982, p. 10). Because of this "Book of Nature" through which God reveals his general revelation to the world, there was little antagonism between religion and natural science. Natural scientists saw their work simply as an extension of their faith. The division that Clarke makes between the Aureate magicians, who could read the "prose of the world," as Michel Foucault calls it in *The Order of Things* (1966), and the comparatively illiterate magicians of the modern age, reflects the more recent development of a disenchanted age.

This inscription of nature in the performance of English magic is not the only significant piece of writing in *Jonathan Strange and Mr. Norrell*. Clarke juxtaposes the imbuement of the English countryside with meaning to another text: the King's Book, a work of magic written by the Raven King in a specially-invented language that has since been lost. The King's Book resurfaces in the novel in an unexpected way, inscribed onto the skin of Vinculus. Vinculus was born with this magical text written on his body in blue ink, like a tattoo. "'I am a Book,' said Vinculus, stopping in mid-caper. 'I am *the* Book'" (Clarke, 2015, p. 995). Vinculus is the word made flesh, a hybrid text that traverses the conceptual division between nature and culture. As a living, breathing text, he exists at the ambiguous intersection between writing and being written. For Vinculus, inscription is not something that exists only on the surface: the *logos* penetrates his being in a way that inextricably links the symbolic register to the material world.

Clarke's novel is also not a single text, but is composed instead of a plurality of heterogeneous texts. The narrative reflects this fact by its various pastiches of familiar literary voices: in "Miss J. Austen, Jonathan Strange & Mr. Norrell" (2008), for instance, Elaine Bander explores the debt Clarke owes to the style of Jane Austen. "Clarke's polite ladies and gentlemen behave exactly as one would expect Austen's characters to behave were they to share their world with magic and magicians," writes Bander. "They speak with Austenian diction, wield Austenian wit, observe Austenian social conventions and manners, and espouse Austenian values" (Bander, 2008). Sylwia Borowska-Szerszun similarly observes that this "combination of two familiar traditions, Austenesque domestic realism and supernatural elements derived from the Gothic, additionally supplemented with a pastiche of historic documents, results in a surprisingly fresh and unfamiliar prose" (Borowska-Szerszun, 2015, p. 11). Borowska-Szerszun argues, furthermore, that Clarke's pastiche of these nineteenth-century literary forms is a feminist intervention in the male-dominated realm of fantasy fiction:

> Clarke appropriates these old-established literary traditions to defamiliarize the form of a fantasy novel, [...] and allows one more voice to be heard—that of an author tired with the male-hero-oriented setting of fantasy. This default setting stems from the history of the genre, whose major forefathers, including Robert E. Howard, J.R.R. Tolkien and C.S. Lewis, were white men of Anglo-Saxon origin, drawing inspiration from European mythology, religion, medieval history and heroic or chivalric literature. Rejecting these sources of inspiration, Susanna Clarke, [...] is free to draw on the tradition of women's writing and forge her own lore and history to "replace" what she finds unsatisfactory for the purpose of her enterprise. Boldly blurring the borders between real and imagined, familiar and unfamiliar, history and fantasy, *Jonathan Strange and Mr Norrell* expands the boundaries of the genre and proves fantasy conventions to be open to creative and insightful reinterpretations [Borowska-Szerszun, 2015, p. 11].

Clarke's novel is a self-conscious conglomeration of discourses, a meta-text that is aware of its own status as a text. As such, it engages

*Chapter 2. Writing, Text, Mythology*

in "creative and insightful reinterpretations" (Borowska-Szerszun, 2015, p. 11), rewriting and reworking narratives that have come before to make the careful reader consider more deeply their meaning and implications.

The past few decades of postmodern fiction have made such experiments with textual form seem commonplace. To rewrite an established narrative, to overturn its conventions through an innovative repetition is hardly a new trick—Daniel Defoe's *Robinson Crusoe* (1719), for instance, is a text that has been rewritten multiple times, from its adaptation as a romantic pastoral in Johann David Wyss's *The Swiss Family Robinson* (1812), to J.M. Coetzee's *Foe* (1986), which tells a modified version the story from the perspective of its female protagonist, Susan Barton. The impression of a text made directly onto Vinculus's body, however, alerts the reader to Clarke's ambition of showing how writing goes *beyond* the symbolic, possessing the "ability to shape and, at times, create a social reality" (Baker, 2011, p. 6). The language of fiction is not just a literary game, a playful sphere inherently divorced from the physical world. Clarke uses *Jonathan Strange and Mr. Norrell* to explore how the prose of the world sets the parameters of how we see the world around us. Stories and reality mirror each other, endlessly rewriting all the texts of the world.

## *The Man Who Was Also a Book*

In the world of English magic, the written word only gradually emerged as a crucial factor in shaping magical ideas that had long existed only as part of an oral tradition. As Davies observes in *Grimoires: A History of Magic Books* (2009), the importance of a magical book often transcended the words inside it. The fact that a book was a material object gave it physical properties that might impress even those who could not read. "A grimoire is defined by the writing it contains, but the act of writing can itself be magic and certain words can have active properties independent of the holy or magical text in which they are written," he contends. "Their power could be stimulated by the ritual use of specific inks and blood" (Davies, 2009, p. 4). The book itself, in other words, could become a mythologized object, as could the very act of writing. Davies argues, furthermore, that the advent of the grimoire, especially after the invention of the printing press, is an important reflection of social and historical changes. "In this sense, grimoires represent much more than magic," he writes in the introduction. "To understand their past is to understand the spread of Christianity and Islam, the development of early science, the cultural influence of print, the growth of literacy, the social impact of slavery and colonialism, and the expansion of Western cultures across the oceans" (Davies, 2009, p. 2). In short, the book functions as a mirror of the modern world it helps to produce.

An increasingly literate culture meant that the role of books became more important over time to the history of English magic. Davies points out that it was the local cunning-folk, for instance, who blended together the oral and literary traditions of English magic. Sometimes they used a book as a physical prop to impress clients, with texts that were large in size, boasted ornate covers, or were written in foreign languages, all features that helped to reinforce the book's air of mystery and enchantment. The printing press provided the most important change when it comes to the history of the grimoire. Not only did printing make it easier to access books about magic, but for the first time it also made them widely available in English:

> Judging from the surviving manuscripts, it was only from the mid sixteenth century that such influential texts as those attributed to Honorius and Solomon began to be transcribed into English, and so made more accessible to those lower down the educational ladder. [...] The rise of printing was a crucial facilitator in the spread of occult works. From the early sixteenth century onwards, Latin magical textbooks printed on the Continent began to circulate in Britain. The key development for cunning-folk, though, was the publication of major texts in English [Davies, 2009, p. 121].

Even books warning against the dangers of magic could inadvertently help in its propagation. Davies points to the example of Reginald Scot's best-selling *Discoverie of Witchcraft*, which provided a major source of occult knowledge, despite its contrary intention of warning readers *away* from magic.

In *Jonathan Strange and Mr. Norrell*, it is primarily Norrell who is concerned with accumulating power by controlling the distribution of magical books in England. He attempts to restrict all worthwhile books about magic to the confines of his private library and, after moving from

## Chapter 2. Writing, Text, Mythology

Yorkshire to London, he is encouraged by Lascelles to begin producing his own publications. Norrell is reluctant at first, but Lascelles persuades him that such a move will bring enough power and influence to allow Norrell alone to set the agenda for magic in England. As such, Norrell creates his journal, *The Friends of English Magic*, to disseminate three basic points to the general public: to affirm that his vision of modern English magic is the only correct one, to police the orthodoxy of English magic by repudiating heretical interpretations of its history, and to attack those whom Norrell sees as his enemies and rivals (Clarke, 2015, p. 146). After Strange breaks with Norrell, his rebellion results in two publications of his own: *The Famulus*, a periodical to rival *The Friends of English Magic*, and the first volume of a book, *The History and Practice of English Magic*. Davies comments on Clarke's evident fascination with the written word toward the end of his study:

> In her bestseller *Jonathan Strange and Mr Norrell* (2004), Susanna Clarke re-creates an early-nineteenth-century England where learned magic once again becomes a profound force after centuries in the shadows, echoing the real, though decidedly less fantastic world of Francis Barrett, John Denley, and John Parkins. Old magic books are central to her clever, gothic re-imagining of the occult milieu of the period, mentioning titles that sound familiar to the reader but are in fact her own inventions. Clarke even constructs her own history of literary magic, inventing the maxim, "a book of magic should be written by a practising magician, rather than a theoretical magician or a historian of magic. What could be more reasonable? And yet already we are in difficulties." This history of grimoires has shown what those difficulties were in the real past [Davies, 2009, p. 282].

The difficulty to which Clarke is alluding here is that, in her fictional universe, magicians did not start writing books until after the Aureate age, when the power of English magic was already diminishing. As such, the authority of books, to which Norrell accords so much importance, is not inherent to the practice of English magic (Clarke, 2015, p. 14). There is, of course, one crucial exception: the King's Book, the only text ever written by the Raven King, the last remaining copy of which was believed to have been destroyed.

This book had not truly been lost, however, for the Raven King's words are tattooed on the skin of Vinculus, "a man who was also a book" (Clarke, 2015, p. 993). The story of the Raven King's book is recounted

## English Magic and Imperial Madness

by Childermass in Chapter 30, when he tells Norrell and Lascelles that this text had once been entrusted to the Findhelm family. None of the Findhelms could read it, however, because it was inscribed in an idiosyncratic system of writing known as the King's Letters, which only a few select readers could decipher. In 1754, Robert Findhelm decided to send the book to Bretton, for reasons that are unclear to Childermass, in the care of a servant named Clegg. This mission turned out to be a disastrous mistake, for Clegg proved himself to be a villain and a drunk. Stopping at an inn in Sheffield, Clegg got into a wild drinking contest with the local blacksmith, which involved a series of increasingly grotesque physical challenges. The contest culminated with Clegg eating the King's Book, tearing it up page by page, and devouring every last word. A few years later, Clegg impregnated a servant girl from Wapping, and when she gave birth to Vinculus, his little body was covered in writing that reproduced the lost script of the King's Book. This book, it seems, is quite literally a seminal text, for that appears to be the only plausible means for its transmission from father to son.

Vinculus is thus a walking metaphor that Clarke uses to explore the growing historical importance of the connection between writing and subjectivity. The notion that who we are as human beings starts out as a blank sheet of paper, onto which our perceptions and memories are then inscribed in a process that forms our character, is an idea closely associated with John Locke's *An Essay Concerning Human Understanding* (1690). Ian Watt makes the influential argument in *The Rise of the Novel* (1957), for instance, that Locke and the rise of philosophical empiricism were crucial to the birth of the English novel, making possible a new kind of modern subjectivity in which the blank page of a person's character mirrors the blank page of a potential work of fiction. That is why the protagonists of the early English novel are all writers in one way or another, whether in the form of confessions, journals, or letters. Writing allows these characters not only to record their experiences, but also provides them with the power to inscribe a new future for themselves. The idea that the old mythologies can be erased and new counter-mythologies produced in their place is the founding promise of the genre.

The character of Vinculus, however, complicates his status as a Lockean *tabula rasa*, a blank sheet onto whom the text of the Raven King has been inscribed. A crucial clue lies in his name, which derives

## Chapter 2. Writing, Text, Mythology

from the Latin *"vinculum,"* meaning "bond" or "link." The word also has a legal connotation, *"vinculum juris,"* referring to a civil obligation that is backed by the authority of the law. Putting these two ideas together, the character of Vinculus represents the confluence of two seemingly incompatible values, freedom and necessity, brought together by the ambiguous act of writing. The paradox that arises from the modern passion for inscription is the discovery that, instead of being a free gesture of self-expression, the act of writing instead erases the uniqueness of the author. "As soon as a fact is narrated—no longer with a view to acting directly on reality but intransitively, outside function, the disconnection occurs—the voice loses its origin, the author enters his own death and writing begins," observes Roland Barthes in "The Death of the Author" (1967) (Barthes, 1978, p. 142). What seems initially to be an affirmative act of human empowerment contains numerous snares and pitfalls that transform writing's promise of freedom into an insidious form of bondage.

Nonetheless, human subjectivity has been irrevocably transformed by the pervasiveness of writing in modern culture. Indeed, it can reasonably be said that the modern subject is one who writes—not always literally, perhaps, but in the larger sense that they inscribe their world, creating a tangible record of their stories and experiences, no longer by confessions, journals, and letters as in the early days of the novel, but through interactions on social media or the mechanical imprint of a financial transaction. In his essay "What is Enlightenment?" (1984), Foucault refers to this feature as modern humanity's ongoing process of "self-production." "Modern man, for Baudelaire, is not the man who goes off to discover himself, his secrets and his hidden truth; he is the man who tries to invent himself," he writes. "This modernity does not 'liberate man in his own being'; it compels him to face the task of producing himself" (Foucault, 1984, p. 42). Here, then, is the culmination of writing's paradox: the apparent freedom of the blank page turns out to be a burden, an obligation, a *vinculum juris* to write and produce. Clarke strategically places Vinculus at the intersection of these ambiguities, the product of both freedom and necessity, writing and rewriting, a testament to old patterns while also the inscriber of new ones: a palimpsest rather than a blank page.

This pattern of inscription is made especially visible in the encounter between Vinculus and Childermass, in which the two characters read

## English Magic and Imperial Madness

each other's fortunes using a set of cards. In her article "The Unlikely Milliner & The Magician of Threadneedle Street" (2018), K.A. Laity undertakes a close analysis of this episode, focusing in particular on how Clarke deploys the symbolism of the tarot. She writes: "Though the deck was not actually called the Tarot of Marseilles until 1930, its occult history goes back as far as the eighteenth century, when 'an occultist named Antoine Court de Gébelin declared [it] to be the remnant of the Book of Thoth'" (Laity, 2018, p. 218). The Thoth (or Theuth) mentioned here is an ancient Egyptian deity, the god of writing and wisdom. In his dialogue *Phaedrus*, Plato recounts how Thoth met with Thamus, the king of Egypt, to demonstrate the benefits of writing, his newest invention. Thoth argues that the ability to write things down and so establish a permanent record would have a beneficial effect on memory, to which Thamus responds:

> Most scientific Theuth, [...] you, as the father of letters, have been led by your affection for them to describe them as having the opposite of their real effect. For your invention will produce forgetfulness in the souls of those who have learned it, through lack of practice at using their memory, as through reliance on writing they are reminded from outside by alien marks, not from within, themselves by themselves. So you have discovered an elixir not of memory but of reminding. To your students you give an appearance of wisdom, not the reality of it; thanks to you, they will hear many things without being taught them, and will appear to know much when for the most part they know nothing, and they will be difficult to get along with because they have acquired the appearance of wisdom instead of wisdom itself [Plato, 2005, p. 62].*

Thoth's mythical status as the inventor of writing leads, in turn, to ancient legends of a magical Book of Thoth, which contains spells to understand the speech of animals and communicate with the gods. In the twentieth century, the English magician Aleister Crowley accordingly created his own occult deck of cards, the Thoth Tarot, with an accompanying text called *The Book of Thoth* (1944).

Clarke gives the pack of cards used in *Jonathan Strange and Mr. Norrell* a further layer of significance by the fact that, instead of being

---

*In *Dissemination* (1972) Jacques Derrida points to this passage from *Phaedrus* as a key example of the notion of the *pharmakon*, a Greek word that, in its dual meanings of both "medicine" and "poison," reflects the ambiguities of writing.

## Chapter 2. Writing, Text, Mythology

written on blank paper, Childermass's cards are inscribed on a haphazard assortment of materials. Because of his extreme poverty at the time, Childermass had been unable to afford to buy paper to make his cards, and so he copied them from the original pack onto an assortment of random materials, such as old receipts, laundry lists, letters, and whatever other discarded materials he could find to inscribe the pictures. Childermass later transferred these copies onto pieces of cardboard, but the glue he used made some of the cards partially transparent, so that the images and writing could be seen from behind (Clarke, 2015, p. 235). As Laity points out, this hodge-podge of random texts "makes the cards a sort of palimpsest of others' words, reflecting in a material sense the weight of history behind them" (Laity, 2018, p. 218). The result is a fitting metaphor of the tangled relationship between writing and subjectivity, for while it is true that the act of writing empowers each subject to inscribe themselves onto reality, the greater truth is that this subject, in turn, is also inscribed by a history of other inscriptions, an archive of ideas, experiences, traditions, prejudices, and mythologies that shape subjectivity at both a personal and a collective level. Writing can thus never take place on a truly blank slate; it is always a rewriting of scripts that already exist. "We know now that a text is not a line of words releasing a single 'theological' meaning [...] but a multi-dimensional space in which a variety of writings, none of them original, blend and clash," notes Barthes. "The text is a tissue of quotations drawn from the innumerable centers of culture" (Barthes, 1978, p. 146). In Clarke's novel, this text is inscribed onto the body of Vinculus: he is the man who is also a book, with the act of writing extending beyond the world of books and penetrating deeply into the fabric of human existence. The parallel is confirmed when the reader learns of the fate of Vinculus's father, who was tried and hanged for book-murder, the last person in England to suffer this peculiar fate (Clarke, 2015, p. 401). This punishment reiterates the inseparability of the material (the physical book) from the symbolic (the book's meaning).

The story of how the Raven King's book came into existence sees Clarke, in turn, borrowing from ancient myths about the invention of writing in order to create her own. The Raven King, upon his arrival in England, was illiterate, since the education he received in Faerie did not teach him how to read and write (Clarke, 2015, p. 398). When he returned to England as a teenager, his youthful self-importance initially caused him to reject writing as a worthless activity. Since his conquests and achievements far surpassed any previous examples from history, the Raven King saw no need to learn Latin simply to read what had others had done before him (Clarke, 2015, p. 398). Instead, he decided to create his own form of writing, a private language that "mirrored the workings of his own mind more closely than Latin could have done" (Clarke, 2015, p. 399). Although the Raven King did eventually learn to read and write in the conventional way, he nonetheless maintained his idiosyncratic form of writing. Known as the King's Letters, he taught it to only a handful of privileged magicians, ensuring its continuing occult status. His book's eventual fate follows a similarly mythical pattern, for as Davies points out, "from antiquity to the present we find the notion [...] that the writing in sacred texts was imbued with physical divine power that could be utilized by eating or drinking it" (Davies, 2009, p. 4).

The story of Vinculus in *Jonathan Strange and Mr. Norrell* culminates with his death at the hands of the gentleman with the thistle-down hair, after which he is resurrected by the Raven King, a narrative arc in which Clarke borrows extensively from the Norse myth of Odin. This story is originally told in the medieval text *The Poetic Eddas*, and involves the god Odin being "hung on a windswept tree" (Anonymous, 2014, p. 32). The purpose of this trial is to discover the secret of writing, which in ancient Norse culture comes to Odin in the form of runes. "Perhaps the most famous tale from the eddas, and for our purposes the most important, is that of how the god Odin hung on a tree, fasting and exposed to the elements, until he was rewarded by gaining mastery of the runes and their magical powers," explains Kieckhefer. "For a divine as well as for a human magician, then, magic is a force closely linked with writing" (Kieckhefer, 2014, p. 53). In her book *Crows* (2005), Candace Savage reveals that there is also a powerful link between Odin and ravens:

> In Norse mythology, ravens had the ear of the warlike Odin, the father of the gods. Having traded one of his eyes for a sip at the Well of Wisdom, Odin relied on his black henchmen, the ravens Hugin and Munin, to fly through the nine worlds and return at night to his throne, bringing him whispered news of everything that was going on. Often the news was bloody—Munin means "memory," especially memory of the dead. And ravens were also associated with the gruesome Valkyries (from Old Norse *valkyrja* and Old English *waelcrige*, the raven, or "chooser of the

## Chapter 2. Writing, Text, Mythology

slain.") Not only did the ravening corpse goddesses flock to the scene of battle, but they could also see into the future, foretell the outcome of the combat, and determine which of the warriors were doomed to die [Savage, 2015, p. 18].

Just like in ancient Greece, where ravens were prophetic birds associated with Apollo, so too they are connected in Norse mythology with Odin, the god of wisdom and the master of occult writing. In this context, therefore, it should come as no surprise that the Raven King arrives to take down Vinculus from the tree where, just like Odin, the street magician is hanging. After the Raven King resurrects his prophetic mouthpiece, Vinculus and Childermass are left alone to decipher the hidden (if suddenly altered) meaning of this writing.

Odin is likewise a figure who has the ability to be written and rewritten, making him the subject of "seemingly endless transformations" (Rudgley, 2018, p. 9). Because of this variability, the representations of Odin are often contradictory, so that he is wise and benevolent one moment, reserved and unpredictable the next. "The puzzle of Odin's multiple personalities does not stop there—he is Sorcerer and Staff Wielder—and because of his shape-shifting powers he is also named Bear, Eagle, and Raven God" (Rudgley, 2018, p. 9). In his book *The Return of Odin* (2006), Richard Rudgley explains the crucial characteristics of Odin's character, many of which bear a strong resemblance to the story of Merlin. The most striking feature is Odin's association with madness, with Rudgley claiming that "the key that unlocks the mystery is to be found in the name of Odin itself. It means frenzy, and Odin is often called the Frenzied One in the myths" (Rudgley, 2018, p. 9). Like the Welsh concept of *awen*, this temporary madness is tied intimately in Norse culture to poetic inspiration. "Odinic frenzy is the inspiration that often overcomes poets and other artists during their creative acts," writes Rudgley. "Poetry was of profound importance in the Northern world, playing a role similar to the mass media of today" (Rudgley, 2018, p. 10). This poetry is more than just propaganda or entertainment, for the words of the inspired bard contained a magic that could reshape reality:

> His role as magician is also related to his states of frenzy, for poetry was also spoken magic. English words preserve this understanding: *enchant* (en-chant) and *spell* both show the link between magic and the spoken or chanted word. [...] Battle fury, poetic inspiration, magical trance, sexual

ecstasy, and drug-induced intoxication are thus all aspects of Odin's embodiment of frenzy and are all altered states of consciousness. So he is the god of altered consciousness, of consciousness heightened beyond the mundane, and as such, potentially dangerous. As a god of altered states of mind, Odin rules not the rational, logic, and orderly part of the psyche but the darker irrational side: he is the source of artistic creation, dreams and nightmares, sexual passion, violent rage, magical trance, and intoxication [Rudgley, 2018, pp. 10–11].

Like Merlin, the source of Odin's magic lies in his evocation of the power of unreason. This magic, in turn, is not created arbitrarily, but proceeds from the cultivated frenzy of poetic creation, a literary inspiration that, with the discovery of writing, can be taken down and preserved for future readers. It is through this revelation of the "hanged god," as Sir James Frazer calls the Odin motif in *The Golden Bough* (1890), that modern humanity discovers that it contains within itself a book, a text that can be copied, written down, but most importantly, *rewritten* as a counter-mythology, a disruption of everything that came before.

## *Writing History, Writing Fiction*

In her analysis of *Jonathan Strange and Mr. Norrell*, Borowska-Szerszun ponders whether Clarke is critical enough in her novel of the connection between magic and the imperial side of English culture. "Mr Norrell's mission to restore English magic fits into the bigger project of establishing British supremacy over other nations," she observes. "These attempts to domesticate magic as an inherently English, not a universal, phenomenon, with the Englishness additionally restricted to upper-middle class gentlemen, dominate a considerable part of the narrative, which despite containing the elements of fantasy does not question the existing social order, akin in fact to that of the mimetic novel" (Borowska-Szerszun, 2015, p. 7). Read from this perspective, English magic in *Jonathan Strange and Mr. Norrell* appears to be part of both the colonial project, and the expression of a problematic national ideology. Borowska-Szerszun immediately qualifies this interpretation by arguing that there are counter-mythologies in the novel that successfully undermine this first, outer layer:

## Chapter 2. Writing, Text, Mythology

If the analysis stopped here, we could prematurely conclude that *Jonathan Strange and Mr Norrell* fails as literature of subversion, which is posited by Rosemary Jackson to be a constituent element of fantasy, perceived as "a literature of desire, which seeks that which is experienced as absence and loss" and opens "for a brief moment, on to disorder, on to illegality, on to that which lies outside the law [and] dominant values systems." Yet, within the second layer of the novel, whose mode is derived from the Gothic literary tradition and clearly indicated to the reader by several mentions of Beckford, Lewis, Radcliffe and Byron, the fantastic escapes absolute domestication, and the parallel world of the Faerie intrudes into peaceful drawing-rooms, taking its toll [Borowska-Szerszun, 2015, p. 7].

For Borowska-Szerszun, it is Clarke's evocation of the literary tradition of the Gothic, in particular, that challenges the English nationalist myth, introducing an element of chaos and rule-breaking that prevents the wildness of magic from entering fully into the service of the state and its imperial ambitions.

A more insightful analysis in Clarke's novel is Daniel Baker's essay "History as Fantasy: Estranging the Past in *Jonathan Strange and Mr. Norrell*" (2011). Baker identifies a qualitative division in the novel between the text's relationship to the realities of history, on the one hand, and the exigencies of fiction, on the other. Baker regards this opposition not as a didactic position to be taken in the name of a higher principle of moral justice, but one that instead needs to be addressed from the more complex and ambivalent perspective of the act of writing:

> *Jonathan Strange and Mr. Norrell* moves between historical fiction and the fantastic, merging seen and un-seen, reflection and reality; it navigates a path through the past and the present, examining the nature of recorded history, while exploring the "world behind the world" and its relationship to the framing of what can be called the "real." Indeed, it is this duality of sub-textual application that has made *Jonathan Strange and Mr. Norrell* such a hard text to categorize, to stipulate genre, to apply a certainty of reading. In terms of historical fiction, Clarke centres the text in England during the Napoleonic wars; populated with characters like Lord Byron and Wellington there is an effort to pinion the narrative to a "factual" history. However, the text branches dynamically from historical mimesis into something more subtle, more complex and

discursively conscious to such an extent as to link both content and style, explicitly pointing to the very *act* and *function* of writing [Baker, 2011, p. 3].

Baker makes the excellent point that, while Clarke's decision to imitate the nineteenth-century style of Austen, Dickens, and Charlotte Brontë inevitably "invests Jonathan Strange and Mr. Norrell with that particular canon's ideological codes, thematic concerns, tenor, and (to an extent) structure" (Baker, 2011, p. 3), it would be a mistake to take her replication of these qualities at face value. Just as the appearance of history in the novel creates a literary double of real events and people, so too literature can create a double even of itself, a likeness that provides a critical distance from which it can examine its own mechanisms. Such a pastiche "mimics, reproducing all that is familiar about its predecessor, while appropriating, subverting and transforming these 'familiarities' to create something different, something new"; writes Baker, "it is both representation, appropriation, transformation and commentary on past forms and their continual relationship with contemporary modes" (Baker, 2011, p. 3). Reading Clarke's novel through Baker's perspective shows the text's duality to be an illusion created by the act of writing. There is *only* the "discourse in parallel" (Baker, 2011, p. 4), the literary double, the text that operates in such a manner that, while possessing the ability to imitate reality if it so chooses, nonetheless remains as absolutely detached from it as a photograph is from its original model.

Like Borowska-Szerszun, Baker attributes the subversive elements of *Jonathan Strange and Mr. Norrell*, at least in part, to Clarke's evocation of the Gothic, especially as filtered through the work of Dickens, but for divergent reasons. Whereas Borowska-Szerszun argues that the Gothic form is *inherently* subversive, so that the wild power of the imagination triumphs over the stolid rigidity of the law, Baker detects a very different dynamic at work. Examining the scene in which Segundus and Honeyfoot visit the Shadow House, Baker pays close attention to the strategic way that Clarke deploys Gothic language and symbolism to create an ominous atmosphere. "Simplistically, such symbols can be read traditionally as metaphor—the decaying, bloody symbology of the rust over the artifice of humanity and the reclamation of human space by the natural world representing degradation in society and a need for change or rebirth," observes Baker (Baker, 2011, p. 8). At the same time,

## Chapter 2. Writing, Text, Mythology

he argues, Clarke is doing something more than just rehearsing these Gothic formulae. There is an awareness in her writing, a provocative irony that transforms this symbolism into "the role of a cipher, being a direct comment aimed at the reader generating a framework for a particular motif" (Baker, 2011, p. 8). Clarke's use of Gothic symbolism goes beyond mere repetition, in other words, by signaling its status as a self-conscious strategy, a cliché designed to alert the attentive reader, through the deliberate clumsiness of this replication, that they are being manipulated.

This attempt to jolt the reader out of their complacency is one of the key subversive elements of the novel, provoking readers to question, through the imaginative perspective of fiction, how the world put before them is implicitly being filtered through ideology. Literature provides an experimental space in which the manipulations of cultural mythology can be made visible precisely because, as a purely artificial construct, the fictional reality in which the reader is invested exists only as a literary simulation. As such, Clarke's use of the Gothic is a way of "demonstrating the narrative process of framing social reality," thus alerting readers to "how experience is shaped by narrative, by text" (Baker, 2011, p. 9). Baker is particularly concerned with how the revelation of such textual manipulations produces "a *certain* version of history" that "is privileged and, in turn, represented," omitting whatever does not fit the mythological narrative being produced (Baker, 2011, p. 9). A text may not have the power to produce reality directly, but through these symbolic cues it nonetheless takes on the "ability to shape and, at times, create a social reality" (Baker, 2011, p. 6), a truth reflected not only by Clarke's novel, but also, for instance, by the repeated historical appropriation of Merlin and Arthur as legitimizing covers for royal power grabs and colonial adventures.

The innovative blend of fantasy and history in *Jonathan Strange and Mr. Norrell*, argues Baker, allows Clarke a greater range of literary devices to disrupt and unveil such cultural mythologies. These fictional elements can be used to take what appears to be a familiar narrative about history, for example, and change it in disturbing and thought-provoking ways to create a counter-mythology. Clarke reflects in one interview that it is the disruptive nature of the past, its surprising otherness, that attracts her to historical narratives. "I don't subscribe to this idea that's going round that what's interesting about the past is how similar it is to the present. What's interesting about the past is how different it is" (Clarke, 2005a). This dynamic emerges in the way that Clarke deploys her alternative version of English history, for instance, placing it seamlessly alongside—and even in the middle of—real events, so that the two sides overlap and disrupt each other. Baker gives the example of how the book's imitation of Austen, in whose novels the brutality of England's colonial exploitation largely takes place off-stage, can serve as a means of disrupting the reader's expectations in Clarke's story:

> That this colonial project and its imperialist motives are left "unvoiced" removes the true horror and depravity they brought to foreign soil; removes representations of slavery in the American colonies, the raping of the African continent. These realities are somewhat blotted out from the historical literature landscape. As a pastiche *Jonathan Strange and Mr. Norrell* is insinuating a line of counteraction. [...] That the idea of war as "fashionable amusement" appears new (strange) *instructs* the reader to receive it in the same manner. Here Clarke takes the elements of Austen's imagery and transforms it. In Austen [...] the action takes place *removed* from the byproducts of the colonial project, its many relationships predicated upon the barely referenced proceeds from overseas exploitation [Baker, 2011, p. 8].

Clarke proceeds in this same "unvoiced" style in many parts of *Jonathan Strange and Mr. Norrell*, a strategy that makes those moments when the novel confronts examples of colonial exploitation by placing "the privileged civilised and the covered barbarism [...] in direct contact" (Baker, 2011, p. 8) even more powerful as a form of counter-mythology. Such eruptions of imperial brutality are meant to shock the reader out of the complacency induced by the soothing myth of nineteenth-century English gentility.

Baker contends that the fantasy elements of the novel play a similarly destabilizing role in the book's critique of how English history is transformed into a national mythology. Anticipating the arguments in Chapter 4 about how Clarke's text functions as a critical mirror of reality, Baker argues:

> The mirror as object and symbol and metaphor is a thing that allows, if not imposes a shift in perspective; a reversed copy that appears, by its very nature, as otherworldly. [...] Here the mirror becomes more than

## Chapter 2. Writing, Text, Mythology

reflection, it becomes a locus for distortion, a window looking both outwards and inwards, a gateway opening out into the un-knowable. Indeed, it is this notion of mirror as conduit that makes the fantastic, as used by Clarke, such a potent discursive mode. The emphasis here is on movement or exchange that flows both ways, between the imaginary and the real, affecting changes in the ways both categories operate and are expressed or represented [Baker, 2011, p. 11].

Rather than imagining a world that is entirely separate from this one, like Narnia or Middle Earth, Clarke's hybrid of fantasy and reality allows her novel to operate at their point of intersection. The world of *Jonathan Strange and Mr. Norrell* is made to appear plausibly close to the familiar context of England, even while fantastical elements intrude to destabilize its mythologies. The "fantasy text" acts "as a fulcrum balancing between what is 'real' and what is 'imagined'" (Baker, 2011, p. 11), allowing each side to reflect critically on the other. The result is not a new mythology, but instead a critical simulation that works to subvert and rewrite the ideology of English history in which it is encased.

CHAPTER 3

# An Artificial Myth

## Dual Perspectives

In a 2005 interview with *Locus* magazine, Clarke recounts that one of her central motivations for writing *Jonathan Strange and Mr. Norrell* was to "explore my ideas of the fantastic, as well as my ideas of England and my attachment to English landscape" (Clarke, 2005b). In particular, Clarke says that she was interested in exploring the cultural mythology of England at a time when the British Empire was at the height of its powers, to reimagine what it was like when England was a superpower. "From an English person's point of view, you look across at America and you get the impression there is a sort of fable, a myth of America: an ideal of what America really is," she says. "Sometimes it feels to me as though we don't have a fable of England, of Britain, something strong and idealized and romantic" (Clarke, 2005b). She recounts that her writing was mainly inspired by examples drawn from modern English literature. "I was picking up on things like Chesterton and Conan Doyle, and the sense (which is also in Jane Austen) of what it was to be an English gentleman at the time when England was a very confident place—as America is now" (Clarke, 2005b). To write such a story about England is to walk an ambiguous line, for there does already exist a powerful and seductive mythology of the English, a heroic narrative that has proven its enduring appeal across the boundaries of both time and culture.

This is the England of King Arthur and Robin Hood, of Shakespeare and Austen, of Elizabeth I and Princess Diana: in short, this whole affirmative side of the English national mythology that continues to present to the world a shining chronicle of virtue and success, a heroic story of nobility and tradition that inspires admiration not just among the English, but also in a worldwide audience raised under the persistent

## English Magic and Imperial Madness

influence of these narratives. This self-mythologizing extends to England's reputation as a place of magic, as exemplified by the opening of Carr-Gomm and Heygate's *The Book of English Magic*: "*The Book of English Magic* explores the curious and little-known fact that, of all the countries in the world, England has the richest history of magical lore and practice," they write. "English authors such as J.R.R. Tolkien, C.S. Lewis, Terry Pratchett, Susanna Clarke, Philip Pullman and J.K. Rowling dominate the world of magic in fiction, but while children accept the magical world without reservation, most adults are not only sceptical of its place in modern society but are ignorant of the part magic and magicians have played in English history" (Carr-Gomm & Heygate, 2010, p. ix). Carr-Gomm and Heygate's willingness to draw readers in through the power of this mythology demonstrates the extent to which English magic continues to be tied to a cultivated sense of superiority that, however seductive, plays a central role in obscuring the darker aspects of its imperial past.

When that mythical curtain is drawn back, as Clarke repeatedly does in *Jonathan Strange and Mr. Norrell*, the history of England is revealed to be far less heroic than the magnificent images projected by its self-mythologization. Much of its "glorious" past has come during an imperial period marked by greed and oppression, so that the brilliant gleam of English mythology sits uncomfortably next to a history blighted by prejudice and exploitation. Indeed, its heroic visions of virtuous kings and their wise "magic helpers," a trope that is revived in the ambitions of Strange and Norrell, are shown repeatedly to be a distraction from the evils of English history. In her essay "The Fantasy of Talking Back: Susanna Clarke's Historical Present in *Jonathan Strange and Mr. Norrell*" (2008), Elizabeth Hoiem draws attention to how Clarke borrows from the fantasy novel's examination of Englishness, a tradition exemplified by Tolkien and Lewis, while at the same time bringing into question some of its underlying prejudices. "I cannot help but note a similarity between Strange and Norrell's flawed project to 'revive English magic' and the creation of 'a mythology for England' associated with J.R.R. Tolkien's mythopoeia," writes Hoiem. "The England of *JSMN* cannot search in its past to discover its untainted origins, because it has so long been an invaded nation of mixed racial identities" (Hoiem, 2008). Hoiem contends that Stephen's final words in the novel are an attempt to rectify this legacy, as he announces "an end to fantasy

## Chapter 3. An Artificial Myth

nostalgia," most particularly "the Gentleman's tradition of commemorating historical events with bloody reenactments" (Hoiem, 2008). The true heroes of *Jonathan Strange and Mr. Norrell* are not its titular characters, as far as Hoiem is concerned, but the socially ostracized figures who play important roles in the story's culmination:

> At the center of Susanna Clarke's historical novel are three characters, each a victim of Strange and Norrell's project to promote magic as rational and "English," and each corresponding to a social group historically marginalized in order to solidify Englishness as a cohesive category of identity: Miss Wintertowne (silencing of women), Stephen Black (silencing of blacks), and Vinculus (the silencing of disenfranchised poor whites) [Hoiem, 2008].

While Strange and Norrell remain the central figures in the novel, they hardly emerge from it as untarnished objects of heroic admiration. Their deeply flawed characters allow Clarke to enact a powerful critique of her homeland that simultaneously mimics and subverts existing cultural narratives about England.

Her depictions of the imperial ambitions of the English, in particular, are subjected to withering doses of irony. England's politicians, for example, are held up as the worst examples of vacuous arrogance, impostors who pompously laud their own virtues by likening themselves to great rulers and sagacious men from history. Clarke relates how the Foreign Secretary compares the current English government to ancient heroes who, despite their virtue, are mercilessly and unfairly attacked by their political enemies: "They were all as wise as Solomon, as noble as Caesar and as courageous as Mark Antony; and no one in the world so much resembled Socrates in point of honesty as the Chancellor of the Exchequer" (Clarke, 2015, p. 81). These deliriously hyperbolic comparisons are belied by the fact that, for all their supposed greatness, the English government appears incapable of coming up with a viable plan to defeat Napoleon and his armies. Clarke further undercuts this rhetoric by showing the reaction of the average country gentleman to such speeches. For this class of Englishman, the kind of "restless, unpredictable brilliance" (Clarke, 2015, p. 81) to which their politicians aspire is a form of educated cleverness that feels uncomfortably French rather than genuinely English. "The country gentlemen had a strong suspicion that cleverness was somehow unBritish" (Clarke, 2015, p. 81). Irony is thus generated both by the disparity between the impotence of the politicians and the remarkable precursors with whom they identify, and Clarke's unveiling of a layer of anti-intellectualism and vulgarity in the wider English population that implicitly undercuts its sense of virtuous heroism. The splendid narrative of mythological gallantry is revealed to be no more than a superficial layer, draped over English culture to conceal the fact that, in reality, it is interested mainly in the pragmatic and unheroic dimensions of wealth and power.

This disjunction is echoed in Napoleon's disdainful remark that England is a "nation of shopkeepers," with its cutting implication that petit-bourgeois philistinism is the true nucleus of its national culture. Despite its widespread dissemination, this quote is apocryphal—indeed, its origins come not from Napoleon, but the Scottish philosopher and political economist Adam Smith. "To found a great empire for the sole purpose of raising up a people of customers may at first sight appear a project fit only for a nation of shopkeepers," he writes in *The Wealth of Nations* (1776). "It is, however, a project altogether unfit for a nation of shopkeepers; but extremely fit for a nation whose government is influenced by shopkeepers" (Smith, 1999, p. 197). To the English imagination, Napoleon is more than just another political threat: he is a mirror image of England's deepest fears about its imperial aspirations, which explains why this *bon mot* about the vulgar pettiness of the English as a nation of shopkeepers was projected onto him. It is also why the defeat of Napoleon is such a decisive moment, for it not only elevated England's standing in the world to one resembling the grandiose myths it had been fostering for the past few centuries, but also represented a psychological conquest over its own anxieties.

> The map of Europe was created anew: Buonaparte's new kingdoms were dismantled and the old ones put back in their place; some kings were deposed; other[s] were restored to their thrones. The peoples of Europe congratulated themselves on finally vanquishing the Great Interloper. But to the inhabitants of Great Britain it suddenly appeared that the war had had an entirely different purpose: it had made Great Britain the Greatest Nation in the World. In London Mr Norrell had the satisfaction of hearing from everyone that magic—his magic and Mr Strange's—had been of vital importance in achieving this [Clarke, 2015, p. 430].

Clarke thus presents here another dual perspective, in which Europeans regard Napoleon's downfall as a moment of reform and liberation on

## Chapter 3. An Artificial Myth

the one hand, while the English see the triumph over France as a manifestation of their imperial destiny on the other. The disparity between these two points of view is presented ironically, heavily implying that the latter reaction is based on self-delusion, a sentiment reinforced by Clarke's description of Norrell's smug satisfaction in this outcome for England and English magic. Clarke underlines the hypocrisy lurking beneath this turn of events for, despite England denouncing Napoleon's craving for imperial power and positioning itself as the ally of a conquered Europe, it turns out this ethical stance was an imposture. In truth, England was hungry to supplant Napoleon not as a moral rebuke to imperial monsters, but because they secretly desired to become one themselves.

The strategy of the English politicians of comparing themselves to illustrious figures from history replicates similar maneuvers by the monarchy, an institution with a long tradition of producing national mythologies for its own ends. A key ironic juxtaposition in *Jonathan Strange and Mr. Norrell* comes from the madness of George III, a king imprisoned in his own palace by his insanity, and the myriad objects and symbols around him that proclaim the greatness and power of his position. During Strange's visit to Windsor Castle, for example, Clarke describes in detail some paintings, attributed to Antonio Verrio (1639–1707), in which gods and rulers bow down before the majesty of the English monarchy:

> The upper part of the walls and the ceiling were covered with paintings of gods and goddesses, kings and queens. The ceiling shewed Charles II in the process of being carried up to eternal glory upon a white and blue cloud, surrounded by fat, pink cherubs. Generals and diplomats laid trophies at his feet, while Julius Caesar, Mars, Hercules and various important personages stood about in some embarrassment, having been suddenly struck with a mortifying consciousness of their inferiority to the British King [Clarke, 2015, p. 441].

Strange also encounters a large mural that is divided between sunlight and stars and features two kings, Edward the Third of Southern England and the Magician-King of Northern England, John Uskglass, as well as Nell Gwyn, an actress who famously became the mistress of Charles II (Clarke, 2015, p. 442). Such an encounter would have been impossible even without Clarke's fictional insertion of the Raven King, since Gwyn lived some three centuries after the time of Edward III, but such inaccuracies are no obstacle to the construction of a mythology. Clarke models her descriptions on real paintings, most obviously Verrio's *The Sea Triumph of Charles II* (1675), which alludes to England's victory in the Third Anglo-Dutch War, and depicts an idealized Charles at its center, being carried in a chariot by Neptune and surrounded by gods and other mythical figures. The other murals that Verrio painted in Windsor Castle were destroyed when George IV remodeled parts of Windsor Castle in 1824, although sketches remain in the British Museum, including one that shows Charles's imperial image ruling over all four corners of the world. This hyperbolic representation of Charles's omnipotence is especially ironic given that, when he assumed the throne in 1660, he was the beneficiary of a political compromise that drastically *diminished* the power of the monarchy. The eventual removal of the Stuarts from the English throne, together with the madness of George III, provide a poignant reminder of the fragility of royal power, a fallibility that the process of national mythologization aims to obscure from public view.

Clarke also depicts how the arrogance of the English imperial mindset permeates the broader population. Consider the example of the Greysteels, the family that Strange meets while visiting Venice. In the novel, the Greysteels are generally depicted in a positive light, forming a genuine friendship with Strange and, especially in the case of Miss Flora Greysteel, coming to his assistance during one of his darkest hours. The Greysteels are not, therefore, to be regarded as bad people, yet they display an ugly superciliousness when they encounter a culture that is not their own. They unconsciously carry inside themselves the self-importance of the English mindset, for instance, when they survey the crumbling magnificence of Venice:

> They thought the façades of the houses very magnificent—they could not praise them highly enough. But the sad decay, which buildings, bridges and church all displayed, seemed to charm them even more. They were Englishmen and, to them, the decline of other nations was the most natural thing in the world. They belonged to a race blessed with so sensitive an appreciation of its own talents (and so doubtful an opinion of any body else's) that they would not have been at all surprized to learn that the Venetians themselves had been entirely ignorant of the merits of their own city—until Englishmen had come to tell them it was delightful [Clarke, 2015, p. 736].

## Chapter 3. An Artificial Myth

Clarke again provides the reader with a dual perspective: a conventional view of Venice as a city in decay, and its reinterpretation through the filter of English imperialism, which transforms this situation into a perverse affirmation of its manifest destiny. The deeper irony is that the true lesson of Venice lies in the opposite direction, for the rise and fall of the Venetian empire is surely an object lesson in arrogance and complacency, a historical precursor from which the English might have profitably learned. Clarke's recurrent use of this dual perspective provides a powerful sense of an English society in conflict with itself, caught between its aspirations to virtue and wisdom, on the one hand, and the temptations of greed and power, on the other.

### *The English Malady*

In the English tradition, magic has long functioned as a diagnostic tool, with the power wielded by a magician providing a moral continuum by which their actions may be evaluated. The historical importance of this function is evident from the large number of magical figures depicted in English fiction and drama, some of whom are referenced in the course of Clarke's novel—Merlin from the Arthurian legends, for instance, or Lord Byron's romantic sorcerer Manfred, a character that Clarke assures the reader was inspired by Byron's encounter with Strange. It is revealing that this theme intensifies in English literature during the Elizabethan era, at a time when the foundations of the British Empire were being laid. The practice of magic, it should be remembered, was not a fictional novelty in Elizabeth's lifetime, and magicians are the heroes (or villains, as the case may be) of some of the finest drama of this period, including Christopher Marlowe's *Doctor Faustus* (1592), Ben Jonson's *The Alchemist* (1610), and William Shakespeare's *The Tempest* (1611). In Chapter 7, Christopher Drawlight thus exclaims: "It is to be quite like a play by Shakespeare!" (Clarke, 2015, p. 100), although Clarke leaves it tantalizingly ambiguous as to what kind of Shakespeare play it will be, a tragedy or a comedy.

The figure of the magician holds an ambivalent place in the English cultural imagination at the dawn of the colonial period. Francis Bacon, for instance, is credited with laying the foundations of experimental science, yet his perspective on the world owes much to the academic practice of natural (as opposed to demonic) magic. Indeed, this line between natural and demonic is what traditionally separates good magic from evil, a division that both scholars and society were attempting to delineate at the time. King James VI of Scotland, for instance, who succeeded Elizabeth I as the English monarch in 1603, published his *Daemonologie* in 1599, an extensive study of black magic. This work was deeply influential, with Shakespeare drawing on its resources in his portrayal of the Weird Sisters in *Macbeth* (1606), a play that mixes prophecy and the occult in its examination of the madness of Macbeth's ambition. It was also a period of widespread hysteria about demonic magic and witchcraft, epitomized by the Pendle witch trials of 1612, which saw ten people hanged for committing murder by means of magic.

While these dangerous themes of magic and demonology are a major concern of Shakespeare's time, this period also shows a powerful tendency to reconsider the past, so that in the literature of the Elizabethan age there are frequent rewritings of earlier myths about magic and the occult. In *Henry IV, Part 1* (1597), for instance, Hotspur caricatures the obscure language of the twelfth-century prophecies of Merlin:

> Of the dreamer Merlin and his prophecies,
> And of a dragon and a finless fish,
> A clip-winged griffin and a moulten raven,
> A couching lion and a ramping cat,
> And such a deal of skimble-skamble stuff
> As puts me from my faith [Shakespeare, 2008, p. 215].

A more substantial shift is noted in Thomas's *Religion and the Decline of Magic*, in which he argues that this epoch is responsible for dramatically reworking modern ideas about fairies:

> So far as literary references are concerned, the peak age of fairy allusions appears to be the end of the sixteenth century and the beginning of the seventeenth. [...] [I]n England it was the Shakespearean period which saw the widespread dissemination of the concept of fairies as a dwarf race of mischievous but fundamentally friendly temperament. It also saw the absorption into the fairy kingdom of the household goblin Robin Goodfellow, who had previously been thought of as quite separate from fairies proper. The older concept of the fairy or goblin as a malevolent spirit, however, was not entirely lost. Bunyan's Pilgrim, we remember, was not daunted by "Hobgoblin or foul fiend." To contemporary magicians fairies were a valuable source of supernatural power. Many magical

## Chapter 3. An Artificial Myth

compilations of the period contained instructions for conjuring them up in order to learn a variety of occult secrets [Thomas, 2003, pp. 726–727].

Shakespeare achieves one of the most memorable of these transformations in *A Midsummer Night's Dream* (1596) through the character of Oberon, a name that "was borne by a demon who had been frequently conjured by fifteenth- and sixteenth-century wizards, long before the title became associated with the King of the Fairies" (Thomas, 2003, pp. 727–728). While Shakespeare is not alone in rewriting these magical traditions, the magnitude of his influence makes him one of the most important precursors for Clarke's novel.

The culmination of Shakespeare's examination of magic occurs in *The Tempest*, a work that places the magician Prospero at its center. In creating this character, Shakespeare draws on the real-life example of John Dee. Dee's rise and fall is repeatedly held up as a cautionary tale in Elizabethan literature, exemplified by the doomed example of Marlowe's Faustus, for which Dee was also the inspiration. "Dee presents a perfect example of the *de casibus* pattern that inspired so much Renaissance tragedy: in the eyes of many, he had pursued knowledge too adamantly and too far," writes Peter French in his biography of Dee. "But he was Prospero, not Faustus" (French, 2002, p. 38). It is Yates, however, who argues most powerfully for the crucial significance of Dee for the work of Shakespeare, arguing that there are important elements of Dee in *King Lear* (1606). "Dee claimed to be himself descended from British kings, belonging himself to the tradition which Spenser had traced, and of which the story of Lear was one of the episodes," she argues in *The Occult Philosophy in the Elizabethan Age* (1979). "Dee in his third period, during which Shakespeare wrote Lear, was banished from court and society, suffered total neglect and bitter poverty, and might well have felt himself to be the victim of base ingratitude" (Yates, 2001, pp. 184–185). If Lear showed Dee at the nadir of his life and career, Prospero is the fantasy of his rehabilitation enacted on the English stage:

> The presence of the Dee-like magus in the play falls naturally into place as part of the Elizabethan revival. That was the world to which Shakespeare had belonged, the world of the Spenserian fairyland, the world of John Dee. He gladly falls in with the revival of the thought and imagery of that world and writes under its influence his most magical play. Prospero, the beneficent magus, uses his good magical science for utopian ends. He is the climax of the long spiritual struggle in which Shakespeare and

his contemporaries had been engaged. He vindicates the Dee science and the Dee conjuring. He allays the anxieties of the witch craze and establishes white Cabala as legitimate. How profound is the change in atmosphere from Lear, the British Spenserian king, abandoned in a storm and mocked by faked demons, to Prospero, firmly in control of his magical island through his white conjuring [Yates, 2001, p. 188].

Unlike Prospero, Dee never did recover from the disgrace of the accusations of sorcery that were made against him. Despite his many contributions to English politics and science, he died in poverty at his home in Mortlake, a broken man.

The power wielded by the magician is a recurrent source of moral danger in these stories, which is why Prospero breaks his staff and renounces magic at the end of *The Tempest*. It is in this context that magic in the Elizabethan age shows a burgeoning fascination with madness, of reason turning against itself, a motif epitomized by the tragic figures of Faustus, of Lear and Macbeth, and most famously, of Hamlet. Shoshana Felman observes perceptively in *Writing and Madness* (1978) how literature is used to explore pressing philosophical questions about the moral limits of human rationality:

> [I]f one turns now to literature in order to examine the role of madness there (in Shakespeare's works, for instance), one realizes that the literary madman is most often a disguised philosopher: in literature, the role of madness, then, is eminently philosophical. This paradox of madness, of being literary in philosophy and philosophical in literature, could be significant. The notions of philosophy, of literature, of madness, seem to be inherently related. And madness, in some unexpected way, could thus elucidate the problematical relationship between philosophy and literature [Felman, 2003, p. 37].

In *Hamlet* (1603), for instance, the protagonist's claim that he is merely feigning madness unfolds as a complex philosophical inquiry that reaches its apex when Hamlet delivers his famous soliloquy that questions the justification for his existence. At the same time, the affected style of Hamlet's approach contrasts poorly with the unfeigned insanity of Ophelia, the authenticity of her suffering and the decisiveness of her suicide providing a poignant juxtaposition to Hamlet's irresolution.

The interest of English dramatists in the workings of madness did not spring solely from philosophical considerations. In the seventeenth

## Chapter 3. An Artificial Myth

century, the living phenomenon of insanity, as opposed to its abstract contemplation, became visible to the English public in the form of the Bethlem Royal Hospital. Better known by its colloquial name of Bedlam, the notorious institution was a psychiatric hospital in London that for many years allowed visitors to observe its inmates for a small fee. "Elizabethan dramatists toured the hospital, in search of inspiration," writes Catharine Arnold in her history of that institution (Arnold, 2008, p. 3). Indeed, some plays from around this period, such as John Webster's *The Duchess of Malfi* (1613), feature grotesque scenes inspired directly by such visits. "Bedlam scenes became popular in Renaissance drama probably because they depicted a single *locus* in which the spectacularity and strangeness of madness were contained," observes Duncan Salkeld. "As a kind of theatre-space itself, a place where comic and tragic fictions of the mind were painfully lived out, Bedlam furnished dramatists with a resource of spectacular material" (Salkeld, 1993, p. 123). In many magical traditions—the story of Merlin, for example—power is granted to the conjuror by madness, and the same is often true for dramatists in this period. "For poets and writers, to be considered 'mad' was a form of compliment," writes Arnold, "hinting not so much at mental instability as divine inspiration" (Arnold, 2008, p. 46). Madness thus became an important motif in the English drama of the Renaissance period, a reflection of its greater public visibility.

While dramatists deployed Bedlam scenes that exploited madness for sensational purposes, there was also a political and critical purpose behind this strategy. Just as the Renaissance stage was imagined as a metaphorical double of society—epitomized by Shakespeare's line in *As You Like It* (1599): "All the world's a stage,/And all the men and women merely players" (Shakespeare, 2014, p. 66)—so too Bedlam, as a different kind of stage, came to be regarded as a double of the country and its politics, reflecting a form of madness that was considered to be peculiarly English. "Madness, in all its grotesque manifestations, appealed to the sensibilities of the tragedians, who could manipulate the distinction between the sane and insane to make satirical comments upon the state of the nation" (Arnold, 2008, p. 45). This kind of satirical mirroring would continue to be deployed long after Shakespeare's time: Jonathan Swift suggests in his satirical work *A Tale of a Tub* (1704), for instance, that since "*madness* [has] been the parent of all those mighty revolutions that have happened in *empire*, in *philosophy*, and in *religion*"

(Swift, 2008, p. 82), the English would do well to scour Bedlam to find its future leaders.

The apparent prevalence of madness in England helped to create the stereotype of *"la maladie anglaise,"* the "English malady." This perception was so pervasive that Shakespeare uses it as a joke in *Hamlet*, in which the witty gravedigger recounts that Hamlet has been sent from Denmark to England "because he was mad: he shall recover his wits there; or, if he do not, it's no great matter there" (Shakespeare, 1998, p. 328). When Hamlet asks the gravedigger why, the latter replies: "'Twill, not be seen in him there; there the men are as mad as he" (Shakespeare, 1998, p. 328). This perception of English madness grows and spreads over time. "By the turn of the eighteenth century, [the] constant increase in insanity became one of the central problems in England: it was spreading and getting out of control," observes Liah Greenfeld in *Mind, Modernity, Madness* (2013). "Throughout the eighteenth century, this increase was reflected in legislation; in the establishment of numerous private and public asylums all over the country, where a few decades earlier Bedlam alone was sufficient for ministering to the needs of the afflicted and their families; in the ubiquity of madness in literature" (Greenfeld, 2013, pp. 402–403). Roy Porter points to several influential books that address this rising tide of madness:

> Through such works as Richard Blackmore's *Treatise of the Spleen and Vapours* (1725) and George Cheyne's *The English Malady* (1733), the nervous, narcissistic valetudinarian became a fashionable if absurd Enlightenment figure. The Scot Cheyne identified his "English malady," a form of depression, as the disorder of the elite in an advanced, prosperous, competitive nation: the pursuit of affluence, novelty, and elegance, and the enjoyment of the "good life"—excessive eating and drinking—exacted a heavy toll [Porter, 2002, p. 83].

Cheyne's text is a striking example of English self-mythologization at its most conflicted, inverting what would normally be seen as a negative characteristic in order to transform it into a positive feature. Madness is recast not as the symptom of a social problem, but as a sign that the English ambition for greatness and their deep moral sensitivity are the noble burdens of their inherent superiority.

The metamorphoses in the cultural perception and management of madness that occur in the eighteenth century provide some of the most important historical contexts for reading *Jonathan Strange and Mr.*

## Chapter 3. An Artificial Myth

*Norrell*, especially with regard to the social changes leading up to the novel's opening in 1806. The 1790s were a particularly transformative decade in the treatment of madness. In France, Philippe Pinel is widely credited with reforming the insane asylums at Bicêtre and Salpêtrière, an event mythologized in Tony Robert-Fleury's paintings. Dora B. Weiner argues convincingly that it was actually "not Pinel but his mentor, the uneducated, humane, and resourceful supervisor of the insane at Bicêtre, Jean Baptiste Pussin (1745–1811), who took it upon himself quietly to remove those shackles" (Weiner, 2008, p. 281). In England, it was the Quaker William Tuke who instituted similar reforms, establishing The Retreat, better known as the York Retreat, in 1796. Tuke introduced what he called a "moral approach" to the treatment of his patients, one that departed notably from the brutal physical treatments to which the insane were formerly subjected. "In the case of insanity, enlightened thinkers thus plumed themselves that benighted religious explanations, and the neglect and cruelty supposedly accompanying them, were being supplanted by reason and humanity," writes Porter. "It is noteworthy that the York Retreat, though run by Quakers for Quakers, employed exclusively secular therapies" (Porter, 2000, p. 217). Because of its location and function, the York Retreat is the likely inspiration for Starecross Hall in Clarke's novel, the private lunatic asylum that Segundus and Honeyfoot establish when their plans for a magic school at this location are blocked by Norrell.

Elaine Showalter's astute analysis of madness in her book *The Female Malady* (1985) highlights how these reforms also reflect changing ideas about gender in the eighteenth century. Commenting on the prevalence of the "English malady," Showalter argues that this concept was interpreted very differently when it came to diagnosing insanity in men and women:

> Alongside the English malady, nineteenth-century psychiatry described a female malady. Even when both men and women had similar symptoms of mental disorder, psychiatry differentiated between an English malady, associated with the intellectual and economic pressures on highly civilized men, and a female malady, associated with the sexuality and essential nature of women. Women were believed to be more vulnerable to insanity than men, to experience it in specifically feminine ways, and to be differently affected by it in the conduct of their lives [Showalter, 1987, p. 7].

## English Magic and Imperial Madness

Nonetheless, observes Showalter, there was a discernible shift in the latter part of the eighteenth century, whereby "the dialectic of reason and unreason took on specifically sexual meanings," and "the symbolic gender of the insane person shifted from male to female" (Showalter, 1987, p. 8). The "moral treatment" instituted at the York Retreat, for instance, is Tuke's paternalistic response to the widespread mistreatment of women in insane asylums, a problematic solution that, in keeping with the sexual politics of its time, was predicated mainly on the perceived violation of cultural norms about feminine virtue.

Showalter also notes how the plight of the madwoman is a prevalent theme in the English literature of this period, and while Clarke makes no explicit references to this body of work, its specter nonetheless haunts *Jonathan Strange and Mr. Norrell*. Clarke's novel is unmistakably shaped, for instance, by the moody influence of Charlotte Brontë's *Jane Eyre* (1847), as well as the Victorian sensationalism of Mary Elizabeth Braddon's *Lady Audley's Secret* (1862), and the themes of female madness that inform them. The work that resonates most powerfully in the background of *Jonathan Strange and Mr. Norrell*, however, is Mary Wollstonecraft's unfinished novel *Maria: or, the Wrongs of Woman* (1798). Wollstonecraft conceived *Maria* as a fictional sequel to her most famous work, *A Vindication of the Rights of Women* (1792), a book in which the protagonist explores the injustices of English society by recounting the story of how her cruel husband imprisoned her in an insane asylum. The fates of Lady Pole and Arabella Strange, the two female characters that experience firsthand the permutations of madness in Clarke's novel, exist very much in the shadow of Wollstonecraft's narrative. Clarke's novel masterfully captures the spirit of the nineteenth century through its pointed resemblances and echoes of these predecessors.

## *Mythologies and Evasions*

What is being examined in *Jonathan Strange and Mr. Norrell*, therefore, is not so much magic as the complex national mythology that has been built around this signifier. In his classic work *Mythologies* (1957), Roland Barthes provides some pertinent insights into the functions of such mythological discourses, and how their most devious tricks may

## Chapter 3. An Artificial Myth

be counteracted. The core of Barthes's argument comes from the structuralist insight that everything in the world can be studied as a system of signs, an interlocking series of paradigms that reflect the values of the society from which they derive. Luce Irigaray takes up this idea, for instance, to examine the gendered nature of the French language—"The masculine is always dominant in syntax" (Irigaray, 1993, p. 30)—that in turn mirrors, she argues, the patriarchal structure of French society. While such insights into the workings of structural prejudices are often fascinating, the real ongoing importance of Barthes's analysis comes from his discernment of what might be called the *insidiousness* of mythology: its uncanny ability to survive its own refutation.

Myths are formed when an arbitrary value is mistaken for an objective fact about the world, so that what is presented as the truth about reality is really a hidden taste or prejudice. Barthes's deepest insight into the success of myths rests on his identification of the importance of the ostensible "innocence" of the subject that consumes and perpetuates these myths:

> In fact, what allows the reader to consume myth innocently is that he does not see it as a semiological system but as an inductive one. Where there is only an equivalence, he sees a kind of causal process: the signifier and the signified have, in his eyes, a natural relationship. This confusion can be expressed otherwise: any semiological system is a system of values; now the myth-consumer takes the signification for a system of facts: myth is read as a factual system, whereas it is but a semiological system [Barthes, 1972, p. 131].

That is why a myth can survive a confrontation with a truth that disproves it, for its success ultimately rests not on the veracity of the facts that confront it, according to Barthes's analysis, but on how the subject perceives their subjective *complicity* in the myth. Irigaray may point out the sexism inherent in the French language, but it is entirely possible for French speakers to acknowledge this general truth while at the same time refusing to accept that *their* speech is inherently sexist. Myths persist whenever a person or group refuses to let go of the "innocence" that comes from refusing to separate their own prejudices from the state of the world. So long as you believe that *your* hands are clean, that *you* are not an active participant in the myth, the myth retains its power.

## English Magic and Imperial Madness

Many attempts to counter mythology fail because they do not understand this basic feature of its subjective structure. It is not enough to bombard the subject with evidence, to highlight the hypocrisy of their position; so long as people refuse to accept such facts as a reflection of their inner truth, the myth cannot be overcome. That is not to say that there is a locus outside of myth, a place of objective truth from which the true state of the world can be reported. Barthes takes the Nietzschean position that all interpretations are inherently weighted with values and prejudices, which render the attempt to be objective or truthful even more prone to mythologization. Indeed, to attempt to free oneself entirely from myth, to be openly anti-mythical, is to become easy prey to the confusion between value and fact that caused the problem in the first place. Barthes gives the example of modern French poetry, which had attempted "to regain an infra-signification, a pre-semiological state of language" (Barthes, 1972, p. 133). "Poetry occupies a position which is the reverse of that of myth," he writes, "myth is a semiological system which has the pretension of transcending itself into a factual system; poetry is a semiological system which has the pretension of contracting into an essential system" (Barthes, 1972, p. 134). In attempting to escape mythology by retreating to a position beyond the manipulations of the signifying order, Barthes shows how French poetry unwittingly reproduced the very conditions it was trying to avoid. "This explains the *improbable* character of modern poetry: by fiercely refusing myth, poetry surrenders to it bound hand and foot" (Barthes, 1972, p. 134). Barthes thus perceptively shows how an anti-mythological stance can end up becoming a virulent form of mythology.

Barthes's analysis appears to result in a seemingly impossible position, a double bind in which mythology triumphs no matter how much it is opposed. It is by learning from this impasse, however, that Barthes proposes a different strategy, one that turns myth against itself so that, instead of confronting the mythical discourse head-on, the critic of mythology indirectly subverts and undermines the source of its power. The key to this strategy is the creation of what Barthes calls an "artificial myth":

> It thus appears that it is extremely difficult to vanquish myth from the inside: for the very effort one makes in order to escape its stranglehold becomes in its turn the prey of myth: myth can always, as a last resort, signify the resistance which is brought to bear against it. Truth to tell,

## Chapter 3. An Artificial Myth

the best weapon against myth is perhaps to mythify it in its turn, and to produce an *artificial myth*: and this reconstituted myth will in fact be a mythology. Since myth robs language of something, why not rob myth? All that is needed is to use it as the departure point for a third semiological chain, to take its signification as the first term of a second myth [Barthes, 1972, p. 135].

Barthes points the reader, by way of example, to Gustave Flaubert's final novel *Bouvard and Pécuchet* (1881). "It is what could be called an experimental myth, a second-order myth" (Barthes, 1972, p. 135) in which Flaubert's eponymous protagonists mirror, through a series of failed endeavors, the delusions of art and science. Flaubert presents his protagonists' world as an ambivalent space, at once artifice and reality, thus transforming it, through a process of ironic doubling, into something "counter-mythical" (Barthes, 1972, p. 136). Barthes's analysis helps to explain how the polyphonic ventriloquism of *Jonathan Strange and Mr. Norrell* creates an "artificial myth," one that both mirrors and subverts the English national and cultural myths from which Clarke is drawing.

One of the novel's most important targets is not originally English at all, but rather derives its outline from the myth of disenchantment articulated by Weber. "The fate of our times is characterized by rationalization and intellectualization and, above all, by the 'disenchantment of the world,'" he announces in his 1917 lecture "Science as a Vocation." "Precisely the ultimate and most sublime values have retreated from public life either into the transcendental realm of mystic life or into the brotherliness of direct and personal human relations" (Weber, 1946, p. 155). Weber's basic argument is that the development of science has produced a rational and secular modern society, in which magic and religion are, as a result, marginalized. The term translated here as "disenchantment" is the German word "*Entzauberung*," and its literal meaning is "the removal of magic" or, more crudely, "de-magification": this "disenchantment of the world" is paralleled in Clarke's novel by the gradual withdrawal of magic from England after the departure of the Raven King.

Although the underlying intention of Weber's narrative is clearly anti-mythical, attempting as he is to make an analytical statement about the effects of science and rationality on the modern world, his description of the world is unwittingly transformed into a myth via the mechanisms described by Barthes: "myth is read as a factual system, whereas it is but a semiological system" (Barthes, 1972, p. 131). The myth of disenchantment, as an account of reality that is inflected by Weber's particular values and prejudices, has become widely accepted as a neutral explanation for how science and rationality have developed in modernity. What is new about this historical narrative is its assumption of an inherent antagonism between the realms of science and magic. The former is now seen as the exclusive product of reason and logic, so that magic and religion are regarded, as a consequence, as irrational remainders of a bygone age. The naturalization of this account of modernity's evolution has been very successful in projecting this mythological narrative of disenchantment onto the conventional understanding of history, even though it is demonstrably untrue. After all, the work of natural science was considered by scientists, from Galileo to Newton, to be a harmonious extension of religion, so that science could easily accommodate magical beliefs like alchemy and astrology. Weber's disenchanted account of the rise of modern science and the inverse decline of magic and religion is thus a perverse distortion of what really happened, yet it continues to wield considerable power as a mythical narrative.

The past few decades have seen the rise of a powerful critique of the myth of disenchantment, exemplified by the pioneering work of Yates who, in books like *Giordano Bruno and the Hermetic Tradition* (1964) and *The Rosicrucian Enlightenment* (1972), shows how magic and the occult exercised an extensive influence over the development of modern rationality. Nonetheless, the myth of disenchantment remains so prevalent that Jane Bennett, in her book *The Enchantment of Modern Life: Attachments, Crossing, and Ethics* (2001), provides a six-point breakdown of the main elements of its narrative that mirrors the basic storyline of Clarke's novel.

1. The story being told "positions itself against a bygone (golden or dark) age when magic comingled with science, God lived in nature, agency was distributed more widely (to include nonhuman animals, natural forces, plants, and rocks), and human existence was meaningful by virtue of its location within a larger cosmological order" (Bennett, 2001, p. 63). In *Jonathan Strange and Mr. Norrell*, this departed age belongs to the time of the Aureate magicians, most notably the Raven King, whose magical powers were predicated on their connection to the world of English nature.

2. Because of its distance in time, this former world is

## Chapter 3. An Artificial Myth

remembered with a mixture of yearning and desire. "Because the enchanted world is figured as the necessary alter ego to the modern, disenchanted one, it takes on a clarity and definitiveness that otherwise it could not have. One rhetorical effect of this is to produce an attraction for this ever receding, but nobly resilient cosmos. Under the haze of nostalgia (or the sway of sympathy for a besieged way of life), the enchanted world becomes an object of longing" (Bennett, 2001, p. 63). While Norrell pointedly opposes the Raven King in his attempt to modernize English magic, Clarke makes it clear that the legendary status of John Uskglass is deeply woven into the English national mythology. Norrell's position proves increasingly untenable, however, and so, as the novel unfolds, Strange transforms into a champion of a return to the ideas and methods of the Aureate age.

3. The disenchanted world of the present age "describes the material world as consisting of lifeless stuff" (Bennett, 2001, p. 64). Whereas the English magicians of a bygone age could communicate with trees and streams, not to mention fairies, the non-magical world onto which *Jonathan Strange and Mr. Norrell* opens seems distant and unresponsive: in short, it speaks a forgotten language, like the rocks in York Minster, whose discourse sounds like two stones being rubbed together while still being clearly recognizable as speech (Clarke, 2015, p. 37).

4. As a result, the present age is represented as "a time in history when the ongoing series of transformations—of demagification, rationalization, secularization, materialization, scientization, mathematization, bureaucratization, alienation—are said to have speeded up, intensified, or reached some kind of logical conclusion" (Bennett, 2001, p. 64). Clarke thus opens the novel with the tradition of English magic at its lowest ebb. The untalented members of the Learned Society of York Magicians epitomize this stagnation, a group that focuses exclusively on the history and theory of magic without ever attempting to put it into practice.

5. The inhabitants of the disenchanted world "are depicted as suffering from this recent acceleration of change, in that they feel the existential pain of the loss of meaning, spirit, or sense of purpose. [...] Whether these achievements are worth the price of meaninglessness, whether the self-improvement and scientific progress that we enjoy are worth the disorientation, is, says Weber, up to the thinking

individual to decide" (Bennett, 2001, p. 64). When the reader first meets Strange, he is undergoing an existential crisis, one that is solved by his decision to become a magician in the wake of his encounter with Vinculus. Henry expresses his surprise at Strange's choice of career, pointing out to him that magic is an idle pursuit that has no application in the real world (Clarke, 2015, p. 257). Henry's response highlights the apparent irrationality of Strange's chosen occupation, its lack of utilitarian purpose making it seem anomalous in a disenchanted world.

6. The final step in the disenchantment narrative "is a twist in the plot, in that fugitive experiences of magic are said to persist within the calculable world. This results in an increased interest among rational, calculating selves in mysticism, eroticism, and other curiosities of the 'cultural' field" (Bennett, 2001, p. 65). This maneuver is the scenario on which the whole narrative of Clarke's novel is premised, so that the return of English magic, together with the reappearance of the Raven King, appears to be the fulfillment of a familiar scenario that has been played out repeatedly in fantasy fiction.

Considering *Jonathan Strange and Mr. Norrell* in the light of this standardized Weberian narrative reveals the extent to which Clarke's novel self-consciously reproduces the basic formula of the narrative of disenchantment. The purpose of this resemblance is not to duplicate the mythology of English magic, however, but to challenge it through the strategies outlined by Barthes. Like Austen before her, who draws on both the novel of sensibility (*Sense and Sensibility*) and Gothic fiction (*Northanger Abbey*) in order to appropriate and subvert their styles, what Clarke is really creating here is an imitative double of the narrative of disenchantment, an "artificial myth" that simultaneously duplicates and undermines the national mythology it seeks to challenge.

Such a project must be understood from inside the logic of what magic means to English culture, especially its historical function as a diagnostic commentary on the ethics of power. For what is the adoption of the Weberian concept of disenchantment but a useful form of denial, the consignment of the sins of England's colonial past to a history that is safely sealed off from the present? Yes, we used to dabble in magic, but that was our former self, before science broke the spell and opened our

## Chapter 3. An Artificial Myth

eyes to the error of our irrational ways: thus speaks the disingenuous voice of a culture that wants to dissociate itself from past errors without confronting their deeper consequences. Norrell uses this same tactic in Clarke's novel to deny the historical importance of both fairies and the Raven King, voiding this crucial history so that he can construct his own narrative of a rational, modern magic in its place. The return of English magic in *Jonathan Strange and Mr. Norrell* is not, therefore, a nostalgia for the glory days of the British Empire. It is an ethical wake-up call, an attempt to confront the sullen insistence that English society bears no responsibility for the consequences of its imperial madness. Yes, it is true that magic has gone from the world, just like the slave trade and the British Empire, but what Clarke makes clear in her artificial myth is that disenchantment conceals and denies, rather than solves, the allegory of power that underlies the English mythology of magic. As such, disenchantment is really just a way of evading the ethical consequences of an imperial history that has irrefutably made England what it is today. To relegate the injustices of imperialism to a disavowed past is, in the end, to insist on a disingenuous form of innocence: so long as you believe that *your* hands are clean, that *you* are not an active participant in the myth, the myth retains its power.

## Chapter 4

# Through the Looking-Glass

## *The Paper Mirror*

As a project of imitation and doubling, Clarke's creation of an artificial myth in *Jonathan Strange and Mr. Norrell* deploys the mirror as one of its most important metaphors. In so doing, she follows a radical shift in the symbolism of the mirror and its relationship to reality that was already occurring in nineteenth-century literature. The French novelist Stendhal, for instance, deploys the mirror as both a metaphor of the artistic endeavor to portray the world around him, and a useful defense against charges of immorality when that depiction touches on aspects of life that are controversial. "Ah, sir! a novel is a mirror travelling down a road," he writes in a famous passage from *The Red and the Black* (1830). "Sometimes it reflects the blue of the heavens to the eye, sometimes the mud of the filthy puddles on the road. And he who carries the mirror in his pack will be blamed for being immoral! His mirror shows the filth, and you blame the mirror!" (Stendhal, 2002, p. 374). Although the mirror is conventionally seen as a realist device for objectively representing truth, Clarke draws on a powerful counter-discourse, already immanent in Stendhal's writings, in which the mirror is reimagined as an instrument of deception, a duplicitous shield for the author's real intentions, one that is rendered all the more powerful by the mirror's ability to *resemble* truth and reality.

Clarke alludes to this deceptive propensity in the magic that Strange performs for Norrell, in which Strange transports a book, Jeremy Tott's *English Magic*, onto the other side of the looking glass. Keeping in mind Stendhal's metaphor of the book as a "paper mirror" (as James T. Day calls it in his study of Stendhal) in which the highs and lows of society are reflected, what Strange achieves by placing one such mirror inside another is especially significant. Typically, a mirror is regarded as misleading because the image it reflects of reality, despite its apparent verisimilitude, is really nothing more than a trick of the light. The mirror's physical surface, in particular, reveals the hard limit that divides reality from appearance, truth from deception. In Strange's trick, one metaphorical paper mirror (the book) is placed inside another, actual mirror, so that even this limit is erased. The simulacrum of the book continues to persist, even after the original object has been erased from reality—indeed, the book in the mirror *becomes*, in this instance, the original, which is why Norrell is so impressed. From an epistemological point of view, this slippage of a simulacrum without a referent into reality is the very definition of magic.

In the real world, of course, such magic is rightly regarded as unreasonable nonsense: the laws of the physical world cannot be bent arbitrarily to transform sand into horses or old ladies into cats. Yet what would be labeled as "unreason" in an everyday context is considered perfectly acceptable in a work of fiction like *Jonathan Strange and Mr. Norrell*. That is because literature, as Felman argues in *Writing and Madness*, can function as a useful double of reality, providing a zone in which readers are able, by means of the imagination, to go beyond the rational limits of what the real world allows. Fiction permits humans a virtual freedom that is otherwise denied to us by reality, an artificial myth into which we may withdraw from reason not for the sake of escaping it, but to re-establish instead a reassuring sense of autonomy in relation to the world and its exigencies.

The apparent limitation of the mirror as a metaphor of discovery is that it is too passive, that it simply replicates, without emotion or discernment, whatever passes in front of it. That is why Stendhal's repurposing of the metaphor is so transformative. His description of the book's narrative as a reflection of what the author sees endows this "paper mirror" with an interpretive dimension that the actual mirror is lacking. Clarke further enlivens the metaphor by making all the mirrors in her fictional world potential portals into the magical domain of Fairie. As such, the mirrors in *Jonathan Strange and Mr. Norrell* are never impassive: their reflections can always be manipulated and transformed by magic. Strange and Norrell regularly use the mirror-like surface of a bowl of water, for instance, as a device for casting visions of far-away people and places. Other mirrors are turned from their habitual functions and transformed into magical doorways. The mirror becomes a

## Chapter 4. Through the Looking-Glass

tool of the magician's art, in much the same way that a work of art may function like both a mirror (which represents reality) and a door (which frames our perception of that reality). This point is made in a scene from the novel in which a visitor to Norrell's library mistakes a painting on the wall for a mirror:

> "Artists are tricky fellows, sir, forever reshaping the world according to some design of their own," said Strange. "Indeed they are not unlike magicians in that. And yet he has made a curious piece of work of it. It is more like a door than a mirror—it is so dark" [Clarke, 2015, pp. 480–481].

The significance of this observation is reinforced by a conversation between Strange and Norrell that occurs shortly after this passage, in which the two magicians discuss a section of Ormskirk's *Revelations of Thirty-Six Other Worlds* that describes "a path which joins all the mirrors of the world" (Clarke, 2015, p. 484). This discovery confirms the literary metamorphosis of the mirror in *Jonathan Strange and Mr. Norrell* from passive object to proactive tool, so that in Chapter 36, titled "All the mirrors of the world," Strange enters the mirror and takes his first walk along the old fairy roads.

The ability to function as a magical doorway is not the only alteration that marks the changed function of the mirror. In the scene where Strange transports the book onto the other side of the looking glass, for instance, the mirror no longer slavishly reflects reality, instead *producing* the image of a book that is no longer there. This opens up, in turn, the possibility of the mirror showing images that are *not* present, to depart from its usual passivity and depict something other than a straightforward reflection. Consider, for instance, the episode that immediately follows Strange's departure through the mirror, in which Drawlight visits Mrs. Bullworth, a woman he has been swindling by claiming he can deploy Strange's magic to wreak revenge on her enemies. In this scene, Clarke describes a mirror that hangs in Mrs. Bullworth's drawing-room, in which the reflection pointedly shows something other than its usual surroundings:

> A tall mirror hung upon the wall above the sopha where the lady sat. It shewed a second great white moon in a second tall dark window and a second dim mirror-room. But Drawlight and the lady did not appear in the mirror-room at all. Instead there was a kind of an indistinctness,

which became a sort of shadow, which became the dark shape of someone coming towards them. From the path which this person took, it could clearly be seen that the mirror-room was not like the original at all and that it was only by odd tricks of lighting and perspective—such as one might meet with in the theatre—that they appeared to be the same. It seemed that the mirror-room was actually a long corridor [Clarke, 2015, p. 497].

The mirror, again, is not reflecting the real world, but instead is "creating" it in an artistic sense. The simulacrum it produces, as Clarke describes it, resembles the tricks and strategies used in a theater to create depth and verisimilitude, an artificial and self-conscious production that functions as a double of reality.

This reversibility of reality and reflection has another precedent in Tennyson's early Arthurian poems, especially "The Lady of Shalott" (1833), the most famous poem from this period of his work. In "The Lady of Shalott," Tennyson subverts the relationship between mirror and reality by having his fairy protagonist sit alone in her tower, looking not out of the window, but into her mirror, weaving the scenes she witnesses on its surface into "a magic web with colours gay" (Tennyson, 2007, p. 9). There is a marked similarity between the Lady of Shalott's indirect gaze, and the scene in Chapter 26, in which Arabella encounters the mad Lady Pole; the latter invites Arabella to examine her Venetian pictures, an offer that is taken up even though Arabella realizes that Lady Pole only ever looks at her in the mirror, never directly (Clarke, 2015, p. 336). The references to "The Lady of Shalott" become more pronounced in the latter parts of the novel, in which Miss Greysteel assumes the role of the poem's main character. This episode begins with Aunt Greysteel noticing that her niece has suddenly gone missing in the middle of a torrential downpour. Anxiously hurrying through the house in search of Miss Greysteel, Aunt Greysteel is startled by what she sees revealed in the corner by a flash of lightning: a woman standing opposite her, a figure whom she instinctively recognizes as the ghost of Arabella. Taking a step forward, Aunt Greysteel quickly grasps that what she is seeing is no ghost, but her own reflection in a mirror. Her relief is short-lived, however, for she suddenly realizes that there had not been a mirror in that location before (Clarke, 2015, pp. 872–873). This uncanny object, Aunt Greysteel discovers, has been placed there by her niece, who has been asked by Strange to use it to help him recover Arabella from the

## Chapter 4. Through the Looking-Glass

clutches of the gentleman with the thistledown hair. Like the Lady of Shalott, Miss Greysteel spends her time sitting in front of this mirror, making observations about the disparities between reality and what is reflected on its surface. Miss Greysteel is also transformed from her usual, outgoing self, choosing instead to spend her days in a chair by the mirror, waiting for the return of Arabella (Clarke, 2015, p. 882). In Tennyson's version of "The Lady of Shalott," it is the appearance of Lancelot that inspires the protagonist to leave her tower, with tragic results, whereas in this retelling the reader learns in the novel's final pages that Miss Greysteel's *father's* given name is Lancelot (Clarke, 2015, p. 985). In keeping with her disruptive use of earlier texts, Clarke's creative "mirroring" of Tennyson's poem is as distorted and faithless as the reflections in her novel's mirrors.

Clarke's destabilization of the mirror as a literary symbol draws the reader's attention to the superficiality of the mirror's function as a device for representing reality. This is particularly true when it comes to the "paper mirror" of the novel form, a textual space in which the world is not only represented, but which also provides an interpretive framework for how readers are to understand that world. Recall Strange's observation, in his ruminations on the similarity between art and mirrors, that artists resemble magicians for the cunning and deceptive way that they manipulate how the viewer sees and understands the world (Clarke, 2015, p. 480). A parallel between the novelist, who uses the Stendhalian "paper mirror" to perform her magic, and the magician, who deploys the reflections in a bowl of water to see visions, is drawn explicitly in Chapter 25. In this episode, Norrell is recruited by the war effort to torment Napoleon with nightmares, delivered each night into his dreams. Hampered by Norrell's woeful lack of imagination, the strategy turns out to be a failure, and so the Secretary of State for Foreign Affairs, George Canning, recommends hiring a team of novelists to come up with something more terrifying. Canning hopes, in particular, to recruit the great Gothic writers of the late eighteenth century—William Beckford, Matthew Lewis, Ann Radcliffe—to provide tales of horror with which to torment the French leader. The plan falls apart when Canning's fellow ministers balk at the scandalous idea of hiring someone so low on the social scale as a novelist, the limits of their patience having already been tested in this regard by the employment of a magician (Clarke, 2015, p. 311). While this episode is a gesture of humorous self-mockery on Clarke's part, it should be remembered that the emerging power of the novel as a political tool to create a world that mirrors English imperial values also belongs to this historical juncture.

That is the argument made by Nancy Armstrong in her study *How Novels Think* (2005), in the second chapter of which she argues that, in the thirty years that divide the beginning of the French Revolution in 1789 from the Peterloo Massacre in 1819, dramatic social and economic upheavals in the United Kingdom redefined British identity in a dramatically new way. "Being British consequently ceased to refer to one's place of birth, native language, or home and become instead a set of obligations and constraints that people could carry with them to other countries" (Armstrong, 2005, p. 54). Through an in-depth analysis of Walter Scott's *Waverley* (1814) and Mary Shelley's *Frankenstein* (1818), Armstrong examines how the novel is repurposed as a tool of nation and empire:

> After the second decade of the nineteenth century, thanks in part to their [Scott and Shelley's] efforts, the British novel could no longer tell the story of subject formation without telling the story of nation formation as well. This mutually defining relationship between an individual and a collective body intent on achieving autonomy and coherence in its own right changed the way readers henceforth imagined both [Armstrong, 2005, p. 59].

For Armstrong, this early period of the nineteenth century is when the novel begins to take on a function that not only goes beyond representation, but also beyond interpreting or framing the reader's view of the world. Instead, the novel is granted the expansive new power of creating *reality* (the title of Armstrong's chapter is "When Novels Made Nations"), of being able to shape and define the boundaries of nation and empire through the act of writing. The pen starts to resemble a wand, passing over a magical "paper mirror" that can inscribe an English national and imperial vision onto the world. With these tools, the novelist's task is not just to reflect and interpret reality, but also to produce it, moving what is on one side of the mirror to the other.

## *The Monarch and the Mirror*

The metaphor of the mirror was, nonetheless, being used in English literature long before to contemplate the relationship between the

## Chapter 4. Through the Looking-Glass

monarch and the domain over which they ruled. Many of these texts are magical in theme, with the monarch, much like the Raven King in *Jonathan Strange and Mr. Norrell*, imbued with special powers and qualities that reflect their superior status. In *Medusa's Mirror* (1998), for instance, Julia M. Walker observes a crucial change that occurs in the symbolism of the mirror from the medieval to the Renaissance periods:

> If the multivalent image of the mirror, so important in medieval writings, has undergone some fundamental change in the Renaissance imagination, this change could be read as symptomatic of the ideological and artistic differences between the two periods. [...] [T]he real change at issue lies [...] in the perception of reflection itself as a mode of representation. [...] Reflection is a reversal, a crossing, a chiasmus of representation between the figure, the tain of the mirror, and the eye that sees the reflection [Walker, 1998, p. 62].

This "chiasmus of representation" produced by the symbol of the mirror in Renaissance literature arises from its new role as the implicit mediator between the gaze and reality. The crucial function of the mirror is to make a subjective split possible even when a literary character, especially a king or queen, is alone; indeed, it is the near-magical doubleness of the monarch, the sovereign and their reflective twin, that is repeatedly emphasized by this conceptual division.

In Chapter 3 of *Medusa's Mirrors*, Walker turns her attention to the example of *The Faerie Queene*, Spenser's epic poem that blends politics and mythology in order to rewrite the founding myths of English identity. *The Faerie Queene* is simultaneously a piece of propaganda and a great work of art, an epic that models itself on the precedent set by the Roman poet Virgil in *The Aeneid*. Just as Virgil's masterpiece seeks to give legitimacy to the newly enthroned Emperor Augustus by connecting him to the heroic legacy of Troy, so too Spenser aims to legitimate the House of Tudor by constructing a mythical genealogy that stretches back to Arthurian times. As such, Spenser's "mirror-filled allegory" (Walker, 1998, p. 70) is populated by multiple characters who are doubles, in particular, of an idealized Elizabeth I, from the titular Faerie Queene to the female knight Britomart:

> As he constructs *The Faerie Queene* with elements of historiography, partiality, preaching, and flattery, Spenser nevertheless gives us an epic that is closer to a steel than a crystal glass. Like the shield of Perseus, however,

> the text itself is a mediating mirror. As we look into the mirror of the text, we may see a reflection of the queen as she looks; but what we see is not the image that meets Elizabeth's eyes, nor can we meet the direct force of her glance even as we look into the same mirrors. Did Spenser hold a common or a crystal or a steel glass up before the eyes of his monarch? Is the glass he offers the same sort of glass he offers to the common reader? [Walker, 1998, pp. 70–71].

The mirror thus functions simultaneously as a medium of representation, an interpretive frame, and, in its deployment of magic, a producer of reality—it is her father's magic mirror, for instance, that reveals to Britomart her true love, Artegall, and during her quest to find him she visits Merlin the magician. Meanwhile, the allegorical figure of the Faerie Queene sits at the center of the poem's symbolism, the magical double of the flesh-and-blood Elizabeth, who somehow combines into a single being the duality of being both an individual queen and, through her reflective doubles, a manifold projection of the Arthurian spirit of England as mythologized by Spenser.

The underlying metaphor that the monarch is a kind of mirror that reflects the state of the nation belongs not only to literature, but also to the history of magic. In her essay "Gnostic Magic in *Jonathan Strange and Mr. Norrell*" (2012), for instance, Paula Brown draws particular attention to the impact of Frazer's *The Golden Bough* on Clarke's novel. Frazer's book began as an anthropological study of religion and mythology, but from its second edition, the importance of magic was also foregrounded. The mirror motif is present in Frazer's work from the outset: the creative spur for his project was a painting by J.M.W. Turner that depicts a scene from Virgil's *Aeneid* in which Aeneas enters the sacred grove to cut the golden bough that will give him access to the Underworld. This grove is located in the volcanic Lake Nemi, about 30 kilometers south of Rome, which also goes by the Latin name "*Speculum Dianae*," meaning "Diana's Mirror." *The Golden Bough* has been enormously influential on how modern authors have woven together literature and mythology: W.B. Yeats alludes to it in "Sailing to Byzantium" (1928), for instance, as does T.S. Eliot in a note from "The Waste Land" (1922), and writers like D.H. Lawrence, Sigmund Freud, Robert Graves, James Joyce, and H.P. Lovecraft have all acknowledged its importance. The central organizing idea of Frazer's book, Brown explains, is that the life of the king has a magical sympathy with the country over which he rules:

## Chapter 4. Through the Looking-Glass

Sir James Frazer described in *The Golden Bough* the ancient belief that the condition of a king is tied to the condition of the land and the prosperity of its people, and the corresponding faith that a violent murder of a feeble king guarantees a restoration of fertility to a country [Brown, 2012, p. 248].

Frazer recognizes this motif in an abundance of cultures and myths from around the world, a continuous cycle of decline, death, and rebirth that Brown, in turn, identifies as a key inspiration for *Jonathan Strange and Mr. Norrell*. "Images of sterility symbolizing the impotence of the English ruler and the sterility of England are scattered throughout the novel," she writes, all signs that England has sunk to a level of decline that necessitates the return of the Raven King and his magic (Brown, 2012, pp. 249–250).

In *Religion and the Decline of Magic*, Thomas highlights another form of sympathetic magic that connects the monarch to the people: the putative ability to cure the skin disease scrofula, along with a variety of other dermatological ailments, through the power of touch. It was from this tradition that scrofula gained the nickname the "King's Evil," although the ability to effect this cure was extended to queens as well. The magical touch of the monarch, explains Thomas, was connected to a logic peculiar to the English throne, in which the king or queen mirrored the will of God, an authority which they, in turn, reflected onto their subjects:

> Faith in the royal miracle [...] [derived] from a belief in the supernatural character of kingship. This belief had its social advantages, for it prevented the monarch from being too closely identified with any one section of his subjects, by raising him to a mystical plane from which he might symbolise the unity of them all. In seventeenth-century England this mystique was diminishing. [...] Faith in the royal healing power was thus linked to a decaying political attitude: the belief that royal blood had its unique characteristics, and a special genealogy extending back to Noah. Kings were not as other mortals, but were accountable to God alone [Thomas, 2003, p. 244].

As Thomas unfolds the history of this tradition, the strategic connection between the purification ceremony and its use as a tool to establish the legitimacy of the monarch becomes increasingly obvious. Just as Spenser's *Faerie Queene* had the ulterior motive of justifying the imperial ambitions of Elizabeth I, so too this "magic touch" could be used to provide physical evidence of royal authenticity.

The first monarch to claim the ability to cure the King's Evil was Edward the Confessor, and the practice slowly gained in popularity during the time of the Plantagenet kings. Under Henry VII a formal ceremony was developed that involved the clergy reading out a verse from the Gospel of Mark about the healing of the sick, with the monarch then hanging a gold coin around the neck of the sick person—this coin, observes Thomas, also gained a reputation as a "magical" object. The restoration of the Stuart monarchy in 1660 prompted Charles II to use his "magic touch" as one of the most visible affirmations of his legitimacy:

> Charles II is known to have ministered to over 90,000 persons in the twenty years, 1660–64 and 1667–83. The peak was reached between May 1682 and April 1683, when 8,577 entries appear in the King's Register of Healing. The numbers were swelled by patients returning for a second time, but the figures are impressive testimony to the rite's appeal. One contemporary declared that Charles II had touched "near half the nation." Adequate figures do not survive for the therapeutic activities of the previous Tudor and Stuart monarchs, but there is no shortage of evidence to indicate the steady prestige of the royal touch throughout the two centuries. James I had scruples about taking part in what he thought a superstitious ceremony, but he was ultimately persuaded to conform to the practice of his predecessors. From 1634 the ritual of royal healing was included in the Book of Common Prayer, where it remained until nearly the middle of the eighteenth century [Thomas, 2003, p. 228].

Although the practice was discontinued after the installment of the Hanoverian kings in 1714, the historical existence of this magical ability is testimony to the prevalence of the idea of the monarch as a mirror reflection of the nation's political health that, as Brown points out, resurfaces in Clarke's novel.

Perhaps the most famous literary treatment of this concept, surpassing even Spenser, occurs in Shakespeare's play *Richard II* (1595). In the first scene of Act IV, Richard calls for a mirror to be brought to him. Despite having lost his crown, he is surprised to find that his face has neither aged nor altered as a result of his downfall, and thus he accuses the mirror of "flatt'ring" him (Shakespeare, 2011, p. 249). Richard then smashes the mirror, its broken pieces representing the inner turmoil

## Chapter 4. Through the Looking-Glass

he feels. The importance of this scene is highlighted at the beginning of Ernst Kantorowicz's classic study *The King's Two Bodies* (1957). Like Walker, Kantorowicz recognizes a shift in Renaissance thought that foregrounds a latent contradiction in medieval political theology that endows, by the magical power of the law, the monarch with two bodies: a physical (or private) body, and a legal (or public) body. Kantorowicz argues that Shakespeare "eternalized" this split, so that "*The Tragedy of King Richard II* is the tragedy of the King's Two Bodies" (Kantorowicz, 1997, p. 26). The mirror scene in Act IV is revelatory for the way it delineates the potential conflict between these two bodies, showing how it is possible for a monarch to be at war with two different aspects of their own existence. At the end of his chapter on *Richard II*, Kantorowicz notes that the reception of the play continued to touch a raw nerve, with Shakespeare's treatment of the machinations of betrayal reverberating through English politics. The Earl of Sussex "ordered a special performance of *Richard II* to be played in the Globe Theatre before his supporters and the people of London" the evening before his "unsuccessful rebellion against the Queen" in 1601, for instance, with Elizabeth seeing herself so strongly reflected in the play's titular character that she is purported to have said: "I am Richard II, know ye not that?" (Kantorowicz, 1997, pp. 40–41).

For all of Kantorowicz's insights into the political logic of Shakespeare's work, his approach nonetheless does not touch on the magical aspects of the mirror scene. In an article titled "Magic Mirrors in *Richard II*" (2004), Robert M. Schuler reminds the reader that the magic mirror was more than just a fictional device. "By Shakespeare's time, the mirror had become 'an almost universal symbol for instruction, knowledge, and understanding,'" he writes, "and it is notable that self-knowledge, which came uninvited with Richard's first two mirror-magic rituals, is now his express concern as he asks for a looking glass" (Schuler, 2004, p. 161). Schuler thus reminds us that, while Kantorowicz's secular reading of the mirror is a powerful political metaphor, magic in Shakespeare's time is also regarded as a serious activity, and that the mirror is one of the magician's primary tools. A collection of magical tools that Dee is supposed to have used, for instance, including a crystal ball and a large obsidian mirror, can be viewed in the British Museum.

It is from the perspective of this late seventeenth-century attitude toward magic, therefore, that Schuler asks the reader to reconsider the nuances of the mirror scene in *Richard II*. "In the Elizabethan imagination, mirrors were associated with three specific kinds of popular contemporary magic," points out Schuler: summoning spirits, identifying witches, and detecting thieves (Schuler, 2004, p. 166). In the mirror scene, he argues, the king must be seen as taking two symbolic steps, "first by deploying his own self-scrutiny as a weapon against Bolingbroke," and then "by turning the conventional iconic mirror of self-examination into a literal magic mirror" (Schuler, 2004, p. 161). For the modern reader, it is easy to forget that magic was regarded as a dangerous weapon in this period. In Elizabethan times, spells and enchantments, especially those directed against the monarch, were taken seriously—part of Dee's duties as court magician was to ward off magical assaults on the queen. Schuler thus reinterprets the mirror scene in *Richard II* in these warlike terms:

> [T]he actual looking glass in Richard's hand also carries literal magical associations [...]. These are hinted at in Richard's apostrophe to the "flatt'ring glass"—"Thou dost beguile me"—where "beguile" means "deceive" but with overtones of "charm, enchant." Richard's looking glass also acquires an immediate esoteric significance by virtue of context. Only moments before, he has taken hold of the gleaming semisacramental symbols of royal power, crown and scepter, and wielded them in striking ritualistic gestures laden with magical and demonic overtones. In such a context—further charged with occult anticipation by incantatory rhetoric and the piling up of Faustian allusions—Richard's odd and extravagant calling for an actual mirror raises expectations of yet another ritual, and for Elizabethans the only rituals performed with mirrors were magical ones [Schuler, 2004, p. 165].

Schuler's interpretation does not invalidate Kantorowicz's disenchanted reading of *Richard II*, so much as provide it with a crucial historical supplement. To the Elizabethans, magic was regarded as something that produced real effects on the world, and it is important to take the intentions of its practitioners seriously. When performing magic, they were not playacting: the aggression of the king in this scene, as Schuler argues, is real, regardless of the fact that he is mistaking mere symbols for reality.

Just as there are two magicians in *Jonathan Strange and Mr. Norrell*, so too there are two kings: George III, and the Raven King. One is historical, one is mythical, but they are designed, in a now-familiar pattern, to mirror each other. As the examples in this section demonstrate, the line separating reality from myth is deliberately blurred. The figure of the English monarch, for all its historical reality, has been repeatedly shrouded in magic and mystification. Clarke's description of the mad King George III, for instance, owes a heavy debt to Shakespeare: "With his long hair, long beard and long, purple robe, what he chiefly resembled was someone very tragic and ancient out of Shakespeare—or, rather, two very tragic and ancient persons out of Shakespeare. In his madness and his blindness he was Lear and Gloucester combined" (Clarke, 2015, p. 445). Royal genealogies have been rewritten so that the line descends from heroic precursors like Noah or King Arthur. Magical powers, such as the ability to heal the King's Evil, are invested in the body of the monarch. Clarke's portrayal of the Raven King is a fictional mirror image of this process, so that whereas the historical king or queen, whose claim to legitimacy is reinforced by these mythological connections, Clarke draws on the devices of literary realism to make her fictional king seem more real. The Raven King is inserted into the timeline of English royalty, for instance, and provided with a backstory that places his origins in the decades after the arrival of William the Conqueror. A key stylistic marker of this aura of textual authenticity in *Jonathan Strange and Mr. Norrell* comes in the form of its myriad footnotes, which provide additional information in a manner that traditionally belongs to serious works of history rather than imaginative fiction. The metaphor of the mirror is what makes these reflective doubles at the heart of English power a possibility, binding them in a contradiction in which the monarch appears simultaneously real and mythological.

## *The Nameless Slave*

The reign of King George III stretched over six decades, from his coronation in 1760 until his death in 1820. This period was marked by dramatic upheavals that have shaped the modern world, including Britain's defeat in the American Revolution, the looting of India by the East India Company, and the inauguration of a colony in New South Wales. The king was also prone to bouts of madness. After he became ill in 1788, for instance, the Parliament attempted to pass a Regency Bill, but failed to do so because the motion required royal assent in order to become a law; the king recovered before a viable solution to this deadlock could be found. A more serious and enduring bout of mental illness in late 1810 led to the Regency Act of 1811, which successfully removed George III from power and authorized his son to rule in his stead. As explored in Chapter 3, in the eighteenth century, insanity was often used as a political metaphor for the state of the nation. Porter analyzes the depiction of madness in the penultimate picture of William Hogarth's series *A Rake's Progress* (1735), for instance, and shows how it formed part of a recurring motif that culminates with George III:

> Is this what the Bedlamites looked like? That is clearly not Hogarth's point: the parable he was telling was about the British. Indeed, on the far wall, a mad artist (Hogarth himself?) sketches a coin of the realm, with "Britannia 1763" inscribed around its rim. Hogarth thus pretends to engrave Bethlem while actually depicting Britain. He is not mocking the mad to spare the sane, he is holding up the mirror to the viewer: it is we who are mad—or, in the words of the moralizing Baptist Thomas Tryon, "the World is but a great Bedlam, where those that are more mad, lock up those that are less." Jokes about mad monarchs came home to roost remarkably rapidly: George III's delirious descent in 1788 provided a golden opportunity for satirists and cartoonists like James Gillray to highlight the craziness of power [Porter, 2002, p. 74].

Porter identifies in these depictions of madness a satirical reversal, in which the inmates of the asylum are shown to be the truly sane ones, who have to be locked up because it is actually English society that is secretly, scandalously mad. This perspective is reinforced by the lingering stereotype of insanity, as we have seen, as a peculiarly "English Malady."

In her discussion of the king's insanity, Arnold argues that it represented an important moment in the treatment of mental illness. "Just as Queen Victoria was to define grief for a generation, the madness of George III influenced popular attitudes towards insanity," she writes. "George's case history reflects the treatment options available for madness towards the close of the eighteenth century and reveals how his condition affected the popular consciousness and led to greater tolerance and sympathy" (Arnold, 2008, p. 145). Like Porter, Arnold also observes how George III's insanity was appropriated as a political symbol. "A mad country, governed—or rather ungoverned—by mad politicians and a mad monarch, England should have been a laughing stock,"

## Chapter 4. Through the Looking-Glass

she writes. "But, mad or not, the nation's problems provided comic relief compared with events across the Channel" (Arnold, 2008, p. 145). The events to which Arnold is referring are the French Revolution and the rise of Napoleon, who headed a regime that claimed to be driven by the ideals of Enlightenment reason. The subsequent war between France and England thus unfolds as a kind of allegory, a conflict between the symbolic representatives of reason and insanity.

The connection between magic and madness provides a crucial framework for understanding the nuances of this social critique. English magic is rooted in the eruption of the irrational, of the advent of a madness that is epitomized by the country's insane monarch: this is the vital starting point for Clarke's evaluation of a society corrupted by the greed of its imperial ambitions, its tolerance of slavery and the racism that underpins that abominable practice, its exclusion and denigration of women, and its rigid prejudices about regional and social class. These ethical shortcomings provide a counterpoint to the fact that the post–Napoleonic period is perceived as the beginning of a golden age for England as an international power, exemplified by its robust economy, unmatched naval superiority, and the expanding limits of its empire. This newfound ascendancy comes at the price of a moral degeneracy that would eventually reflect the empire's downfall.

The insane figure of King George III captures the ambiguity of this legacy and distills it into a single, symbolic figure. The king holds within himself an opposing set of contradictory positions that, at their extremes, mirror each other. As the sovereign monarch of Britain, on the one hand, he is a figure of power, the word "sovereign" referring not only to his political authority but also to a radical freedom that sets him apart from the limitations that bind the common people. On the other hand, madness makes dramatically transparent the public restrictions of the king's office, so that, while still bearing the formal title of sovereign, George III is transformed into a prisoner of his condition, as Strange witnesses during his visit to the palace (Clarke, 2015, p. 445). His mind ruined by madness, the king loses his sovereignty in a dual sense, for insanity robs him of both his personal autonomy and his political authority. Only the formal shell of his status remains, and so it is that Kantorowicz's insightful analysis reveals how the personal body can be held prisoner by the legal body: the former, in effect, becomes the nameless slave of the latter.

## English Magic and Imperial Madness

In Clarke's depiction of the mad king, George III latches onto the magical idea that his fate is connected with the wellbeing of the nation. The king thus regards the physical torment of the treatments administered by his physicians, the brothers John and Robert Willis, to be a suffering that is inflicted not only on himself, but an anguish that, in an echo of Frazer's thesis, is mirrored by the country as a whole. When Strange and George III escape from the clutches of the Willises with the aid of some fairy magic, for instance, the king tells Strange that he "was convinced that a great many disasters had befallen Great Britain since he had become mad. He seemed to imagine that the wreck of his own reason must be matched by a corresponding wreck of the kingdom" (Clarke, 2015, p. 459). The king's delusion comes from taking the mythologies of the English royal house seriously—the prophecies, the healing touch, the heroic genealogies—so that he quixotically sees himself as a character in a play, talking "incessantly for hours, telling endless anecdotes about people who had long since died, discussing his own illness and reciting the mad scenes from *King Lear* or the blindness of Milton's *Samson Agonistes*" (Arnold, 2008, p. 156). The emptiness of this rhetoric is demonstrated shortly afterward, during the brief sojourn into Faerie:

> Strange [...] escorted His Majesty through several rooms. All had painted ceilings in which English monarchs were depicted as dashing about the sky in fiery chariots, vanquishing persons who symbolized Envy, Sin and Sedition, and establishing Temples of Virtue, Palaces of Eternal Justice and other useful institutions of that sort. But though the ceilings were full of the most intense activity, the rooms beneath them were forlorn, threadbare and full of dust and spiders. The furniture was all covered up with sheets so that it appeared as if these chairs and tables must have died some time ago and these were their gravestones [Clarke, 2015, p. 451].

The king of England is caught in a delusion that inverts fiction and reality, the fulfillment of Jacques Lacan's famous observation that if "a man who thinks he is a king is mad, a king who thinks he is a king is no less so" (Lacan, 2006, p. 139). To be a king is to occupy a symbolic role, so that only someone who mistakes the symbol for reality, such as a Quixote, can take its meaning seriously.

In his madness, the king never lapses into outright nonsense, for his words always possess some latent meaning or sense. Indeed, one of the

## Chapter 4. Through the Looking-Glass

grimly amusing aspects of Clarke's representation of George III is how she places fragments of Enlightenment reason into his mouth. Consider, for instance, these words that the king utters to Strange: "'But how do I know that you are not a wicked demon come to tempt me?' he asked at last in a tone of the most complete reasonableness" (Clarke, 2015, p. 450). The king's seemingly random words are a pointed allusion to a passage from René Descartes's *Meditations* (1641) in which the philosopher considers the possibility that an evil demon is falsifying his every perception. "Therefore, I will suppose that, not God who is the source of truth but some evil mind, who is all powerful and cunning, has devoted all their energies to deceiving me," writes Descartes. "I will imagine that the sky, air, earth, colours, shapes, sounds and everything external to me are nothing more than the creatures of dreams by means of which an evil spirit entraps my credulity" (Descartes, 2003, p. 22). This famous thought experiment, as we shall see in Chapter 6, was a key part of the debate between Foucault and Derrida about the historical configuration of madness.

The most poignant thing that the king says comes during the conversation he is holding with an "imaginary silver-haired person," a figure who is evidently the gentleman with the thistledown hair (Clarke, 2015, p. 448). The gentleman is the ruler of Lost-hope, a kingdom in the land of Faerie, and for that reason he sees himself as the social equal of George III:

> "I beg your pardon for mistaking you for a common person," he said.
> "You may be a king just as you say, but I merely take the liberty of observing that I have never heard of any of your kingdoms. Where is Lost-hope? Where are the Blue Castles? Where is the City of Iron Angels? I, on the other hand, am King of *Great Britain*, a place everyone knows and which is clearly marked on all the maps!" [Clarke, 2015, p. 448].

This last statement is replete with irony, for thanks to the interventions of Geoffrey of Monmouth, Dee, and others, the map of Great Britain, especially the founding notion that the limits of its empire were originally defined in the days of King Arthur, is truly as rooted in magic and mythology as any of the fairy kingdoms.

The reader is not privy to what the gentleman says next, but it can be deduced from the king's response that it relates to the fairy's stated intention of overthrowing England's current ruler and installing Stephen in his place. The king replies: "Pray, do not be angry! You are a king and I am a king! We shall all be kings together!" (Clarke, 2015, p. 448). The possibility that Stephen might be the new King of England establishes him as a second double of George III. Stephen experiences constant racism because of his appearance, yet his personal qualities are such that he manages to rise to the position of butler in Walter Pole's household, his success and charisma causing people to speculate behind his back that he actually comes from a royal family in Africa:

> [A] rumour had been circulating London for years to the effect that Stephen Black was not really a butler at all. Secretly he was an African prince, the heir to a vast kingdom, and it was well known that as soon as he grew tired of being a butler he would return there and marry a princess as black as himself. After this revelation the Harley-street servants watched Stephen out of the corners of their eyes and agreed among themselves that nothing was more likely. In fact, was not their own obedience to Stephen the best proof of it? For it was hardly likely that such independent, proud-spirited Englishmen and women would have submitted to the authority of a *black man*, had they not instinctively felt that respect and reverence which a commoner feels for a king! [Clarke, 2015, pp. 175–176].

The covert prejudices that these everyday English people feel toward Stephen are accentuated by the fairy's protective magic, which transforms any negative actions against him into unwitting gestures of benevolence. Stephen thus experiences the ideology of the free and sovereign English subject as a cruel invention, a purported principle of justice from which only he, it seems, has been perversely excepted.

As the gentleman with the thistledown hair progresses with his plan to place Stephen on the English throne, Stephen is forced to confront those imperial injustices in which George III is a central historical player. For most of George's reign, for instance, the African slave trade was one of the country's most lucrative business ventures. Although England lost its American colonies, the Caribbean possessions, which is where Stephen was conceived, were seen by the English as having far greater strategic importance. Religious and political factors led to the creation of the Committee for the Abolition of the Slave Trade in 1787, which in turn instituted the Slave Trade Act of 1807, outlawing the slave trade in the British Empire and establishing the legal position that slavery was illegal on home soil. When the gentleman with the

## Chapter 4. Through the Looking-Glass

thistledown hair suggests that Stephen should revenge himself on the "wicked English" (Clarke, 2015, p. 404) for enslaving Stephen and his mother, Stephen replies in their defense: "No one who stands on British soil can be a slave. The air of England is the air of liberty. It is a great boast of Englishmen that this is so" (Clarke, 2015, p. 404). These spoken words are then supplemented by an unspoken, subversive thought: "*And yet*, he thought, *they own slaves in other countries*" (Clarke, 2015, p. 404). When they are together, Stephen recurrently presents the gentleman with the thistledown hair with this kind of measured, reasonable response. Yet it is precisely the manic unreason of the fairy that brings out this critical side in Stephen, revealing how the ugliness of English racism is the inversion of its more presentable façade of respectability and moral righteousness.

The gentleman with the thistledown hair is the one who takes Stephen through the looking glass, who forces him to enter Faerie and so regard English society through the critical lens of unreason. To this end, Clarke accentuates the mirror symbolism when the fairy first encounters Stephen, placing the two side-by-side in a revelatory meeting, in which the gentleman with the thistledown hair sees Stephen's potential and articulates a plan to elevate him to the monarchy. In that moment, the fairy and Stephen stand together and admire each other in the mirror, the latter's handsome features and commanding mien causing the gentleman with the thistledown hair to assert that Stephen's position as a servant is a miscarriage of justice, one that the fairy will rectify by restoring Stephen to his rightful status as a king (Clarke, 2015, pp. 187–188). Clarke thus highlights the hypocrisy of English society by making Stephen Black and King George III, despite occupying opposite ends of the social scale, into mirror images of one another. Both characters are cruelly tormented by the hypocrisy of a society that outwardly proclaims its rational ideal of individual freedom, but then negates that freedom through a series of ingrained prejudices. This vanishing act is the unhappy essence of English magic, the reverse alchemical ability to transform the gold of reason into the base metal of unreason. Despite its apparent lack of value, however, Clarke's book demonstrates that even this base metal may be polished until it finds a new function as a looking glass, a brilliant surface that novelist can once again carry down the road to reflect either the beauty of the heavens above, or the mud on the path below.

## Chapter 5

# Imperialism's Magic Helper

## *Anthropology and Unreason*

The presence of Stephen Black in *Jonathan Strange and Mr. Norrell* is a poignant reminder of the racism that underlies the construction of Englishness and its imperial ambitions. "Clarke is bearing witness to the reality of black people in Britain in the early 1800s," observes Birns. "By having Black so intimately involved in a plot concerning the restoration of English magic, Clarke is also urging the reader to consider black Britishness as part of the very concept of England itself" (Birns, 2020, p. 125). In a society where the markers of social status are the external prompts for how a person ought to be treated, Stephen's expensive clothing and gentlemanly manners are repeatedly trumped by the color of his skin. When Stephen accidentally bumps into a gentleman wearing a blue coat on the street, for instance, the latter immediately assumes that he is under attack (Clarke, 2015, p. 201). "Would an English jury be able to conceive of a black man who did not steal and lie?" ponders Stephen, as he watches this response with resigned detachment. "A black man who was a respectable person? It did not seem very likely" (Clarke, 2015, p. 201). Stephen is saved from reprisal by the intervention of fairy magic, a protection spell that turns the gentleman in the blue coat into a tree. Nonetheless, the artificial run of good luck that Stephen experiences from this protection spell only highlights the depth of the prejudices that form a constant obstacle in his life.

When Stephen meets Vinculus later in the novel, he reflects further on how his skin color evokes racist responses from the English people around him. These thoughts are elicited by the fact that, while Vinculus's face is unmarked, the rest of the street magician's body is covered in blue ink, tattoos that were magically inscribed on his body at birth:

## English Magic and Imperial Madness

>Stephen hesitated. "Your skin is marked and discoloured. I thought perhaps the marks meant you had a disease of some sort."
>
>"That is not what my skin means," said Vinculus.
>
>"Means?" said Stephen. "That is an odd word to use. Yet it is true—skin can mean a great deal. Mine means that any man may strike me in a public place and never fear the consequences. It means that my friends do not always like to be seen with me in the street. It means that no matter how many books I read, or languages I master, I will never be any thing but a curiosity—like a talking pig or a mathematical horse" [Clarke, 2015, p. 677].

In this example, Clarke draws together the human body and the act of writing, showing how, together, they participate in a symbolic hierarchy in which the sign eclipses what it represents. The sign in question—the blackness of Stephen's skin—triggers a script, a mythology that judges him, unreasonably, by a symbolic rubric rather than by the reality of who he is. A pressing question that Clarke's novel requires us to consider, therefore, is how this racist script came to be written and disseminated.

While there is no shortage of books aiming to provide an answer to this complex historical question, this chapter examines this problem from the perspective of English magic: in short, what part does magic play in the writing of English magic's racist script? The starting point for this investigation comes from a line in Graham M. Jones's *Magic's Reason: An Anthropology of Analogy* (2017), in which he states: "British anthropology helped create 'the idea of Englishness' by theorizing African kinship in a way that made English kinship appear distinctive" (Jones, 2017, p. 142). Critics working in this field agree that the anthropologists of the nineteenth and early twentieth centuries were instrumental in the modern establishment of a colonial and racist interpretation of the practice of magic. Indeed, Jones structures his book around the dual poles of magic and anthropology, examining how each discourse has shaped the other: "My argument is largely organized around tracing the legacies of two figures, the French illusionist Jean-Eugène Robert-Houdin (1805–1871) and the English anthropologist Sir Edward Burnett Tylor (1832–1917)" (Jones, 2017, p. 7). What was at stake in the anthropological divisions of modern and primitive, scientific and magical, European and African, boiled down to what was considered rational. "Somehow Europeans (but not Africans, presumably)

## Chapter 5. Imperialism's Magic Helper

can still be seen as gullible," writes Susan Greenwood in *The Anthropology of Magic* (2009). "When it comes to issues of magic, the rationalism (and racism) inherent in anthropological discourse needs to be recognised and avoided" (Greenwood, 2009, p. 5). It is in this anthropological context, therefore, that the split between reason and unreason takes on a concrete political meaning.

The key works from this anthropological tradition belong to only a handful of influential thinkers—Tylor's *Primitive Culture* (1871), Frazer's *The Golden Bough*, and Henry Hubert and Marcel Mauss's *A General Theory of Magic* (1902) are the chief examples—yet the ideas expressed in these texts have been echoed repeatedly by both their contemporaries and later thinkers. As Robert J. Wallis outlines in "Witchcraft and Magic in the Age of Anthropology" (2017), the Victorian anthropologists claimed to be undertaking a scientific study of "primitive" culture:

> In their work, both Tylor and Frazer used the categories of magic, science, and religion to organize their thinking. They both thought that belief in witchcraft and magic in "primitive" societies were "survivals" from prehistoric times, and that these fossils of "superstition" evidenced a ladder of progress by which cultures develop from "savagery" to "civilization," with religions developing from animism through totemism and polytheism to monotheism. "Magic," as a superstitious practice, was destined to die out, but remained of interest to science as a relic of primitive practices and therefore worthy of collection, record, and study [Wallis, 2017, p. 229].

Wallis points out that these anthropologists were influenced by breakthroughs in other scientific fields like geology and biology, with Charles Darwin's ideas about evolution, in particular, being imported by analogy into the anthropological understanding of culture. The result, argues Wallis, was a discourse that was not only inherently ethnocentric, ignoring the complexities of the indigenous cultures that were being studied, but also wildly erroneous, insofar as culture simply does not follow the same rules as biological evolution. "Neither technological determinism (improvements in technology, from stone to metal tools, for example) nor cultural Darwinism (that certain cultures are unable to progress and so will become extinct—a racist, incorrect, if still prevalent notion)" provide accurate or satisfactory descriptions of how a culture changes over time (Wallis, 2017, p. 229).

The advent of a critique of colonialism and its legacy over the past few decades has led to a reassessment of the underlying racism and cultural prejudices of anthropology as a discipline. Nonetheless, many writers working in this field note that there are persistent structural biases when it comes to the association of magic with "backward" and "primitive" cultures. When Greenwood was writing *The Anthropology of Magic*, for instance, she noticed that magic and witchcraft were studied by anthropologists primarily as an African phenomenon, so that "while much has been written about African witchcraft and magic, much less attention has been given to Western approaches" (Greenwood, 2009, p. 2). Greenwood also notices a qualitative difference in how magical traditions are framed, depending on their point of origin:

> [T]here is currently a tremendous surge of anthropological interest in magic in Western cultures, which is largely due to its use as an analytical category to elucidate a wide variety of processes and practices to do with modernity. *Magic* covers a repertoire of related terms and has versatility and plasticity; in the past, it has been used as a vague marker of otherness that freezes non–Western subjects in premodern time, but it is now increasingly being employed as a counterpoint to liberal understandings of modernity's rational progress [Greenwood, 2009, p. 2].

Despite being purged of its explicit racism, in other words, anthropology retains many racist prejudices at a structural level. Because African cultures were assumed by earlier anthropologists to be inherently irrational and superstitious, the existence of magic in them was presented as natural, in contrast to the superior rationality of Western culture, where it is regarded as a marginal activity. This dichotomy remains largely intact, for the resurgent interest in magic in the West, despite contradicting the basic tenets of Tylor and Frazer's arguments about rational progress eliminating magic and superstition, is never presented as unreasonable, but rather as a measured critique of the excesses of disenchanted reason. Even in its unreason, Western culture insists on maintaining the appearance of remaining within the fold of reason, while continuing to exclude non–Western cultures from it.

Randall Styers makes a comparable argument in his book *Making Magic: Religion, Magic, and Science in the Modern World* (2004), in which he confirms the overwhelming tendency to treat magic as a non–Western phenomenon. "Even scholars who acknowledged that magic was more widespread and pervasive than this narrow attribution," he writes, "regularly restricted their consideration of magic to its

## Chapter 5. Imperialism's Magic Helper

preliterate and non–Western manifestations (offering disclaimers to the effect that magic is particularly 'well exemplified in rude communities')" (Styers, 2004, p. 14). Similarly, there has been a mutation of the language of prejudice in the anthropological discourse about magic, Styers argues, a retreat into euphemism that preserves the discipline's racist and colonial assumptions by enacting what outwardly looks like a correction, but which is really only an act of concealment. "[C]ontemporary theories of magic still often invoke these earlier traditions [...] either through the very structure of their analysis or through other types of scholarly sleight of hand," writes Styers. "While it might appear unseemly to speak of 'primitives,' it remains perfectly acceptable to speak of 'magic in the life of traditional peoples'; there is little ambiguity as to who constitutes a 'traditional' person and who does not" (Styers, 2004, p. 14). The anthropological discussion of magic thus plays a crucial role in writing the racist script that underpins English colonialism:

> This link of magic with the "primitive" underscores one of the most important functions of scholarly discourse on magic. These theories served through much of the past century as an important ideological tool in the aid of European and American imperialism and colonialism. Theories of magic confirmed that the mental processes of nonmodern, non–Western peoples are benighted and superstitious[.] [...] A propensity to magic demonstrates an incapacity for responsible self-government; people prone to magic call out for enlightened control. Euro-American imperialism has commonly been overlaid with a religious mission, and this missionizing theme has been prominent in theoretical texts concerning magic [Styers, 2004, p. 14].

The implicit critique in *Jonathan Strange and Mr. Norrell* rests on a similar willingness to examine the hidden prejudices of its fictional architecture. By drawing attention to its own construction, Clarke's novel asks the reader, in turn, also to take notice of the discourses that have been assembled to structure the notion of English magic: an imperial discourse of "Englishness," which is underpinned by a definition of rationality and disenchantment that conceals an ugly history of racism and prejudice.

## *The Illusionist's Mission*

The extent to which magic, through the influence of these anthropological ideas, has become entangled in the discourse of European colonization can be seen in the cultural development of what Simon During refers to as "secular magic." In his book *Modern Enchantments: The Cultural Power of Secular Magic* (2002), During makes a formal distinction between occult magic and secular magic, the latter being "the technically produced magic of conjuring shows and special effects" that "stakes no serious claim to contact with the supernatural" (During, 2002, p. 1). During concurs that anthropology had a major role in defining the reception of both kinds of magic, once again using the assumption of Western rationality as its underlying basis. "These works systematized the magic/reason opposition and inserted it into an implicitly colonialist theory of history and society," he writes. "This was based on the claim that the mentalities of 'savages' (that is, colonizable peoples) and the 'civilized' (that is, their colonizers) were as different from one another other as magic is from reason, even if they were not always fundamentally discontinuous" (During, 2002, p. 16). By focusing on secular (or stage) magic, During provides a further twist on this familiar discourse, for secular magic's emphasis on technical skill in creating its illusions, together with its rejection of a supernatural basis, produces a disenchanted variation of the Norrellite dream: a form of magic that is altogether rational and, as a result, aspires to respectability.

During's study is exceptional in its focus on secular magic, for while there is a long history of scholarship on the occult, few others have written about the more commonplace art of illusion and sleight-of-hand. The critic who follows most closely in During's footsteps is Jones, whose pairing of Robert-Houdin and Tylor further reinforces the tie that During establishes between anthropology and secular magic. Indeed, of the two critics, it is perhaps Jones, himself an Associate Professor of Anthropology at MIT, who delves into this connection in more depth and detail. Jones reveals that part of his motivation in investigating this link came from encountering the attitudes of contemporary illusionists and secular magicians that he met. In a reflection of the ongoing influence of Victorian anthropology, Jones noticed that many of these people believed that there was an inherent historical continuity linking occult to secular magic, that the latter practice grew out of a version of the former. "Among magicos, it was nearly a truism that entertainment magic derived from occult magic, or at least that there was a relationship, if not of ancestry, then of family resemblance that bound the figures of the occult, instrumental magician and the secular, entertainment magician

## Chapter 5. Imperialism's Magic Helper

conceptually together," he writes. "There are a variety of deep historical reasons why magicos would associate illusionistic and instrumental magic" (Jones, 2017, p. 9). The nucleus of this view, of course, is the Weberian narrative of disenchantment, the notion that magic can only be allowed to exist in the modern world if it discards its mystical aspects and submits to the parameters of the rational.

This interplay between the occult and secular magic has a long history, with the opposing sides sometimes engaged in direct conflict with each other. The invention of the printing press, for instance, led to the widespread distribution of manuals that showed readers how magic tricks and illusions were performed, allowing secular magicians to "disenchant" the claims of the occult to mystical or supernatural knowledge. Secular magic has thus frequently functioned as a mirror image of the occult, its rational double, so that "entertainment-and-fictional fictional magic refers back to its 'real' double even when departing from it," as During argues. "Thus the logic of secular magic is describable only in relation to a magic with supernatural purpose" (During, 2002, p. 3). This ambiguous relationship between the two forms of magic becomes especially important when considering the cultural reception of secular magicians. In Chapter 4 of *Modern Enchantments*, During contends that the overwhelming predominance in the nineteenth century of magicians who were white and male reflected new cultural anxieties about imperial superiority. As a result, the possibility that non-white magicians might trick a white audience became a political statement, an implicit challenge to the racist colonial order that could not be tolerated. During also contends that secular magic could never truly shake its association with the supernatural. In the minds of such audiences, non-white magicians were closely associated with "black" (that is to say, evil) magic, while female magicians brought back haunting cultural memories of witches:

> The fact that enlightened conjurers were still associated, more or less subliminally, with occult or supernatural agency posed a major difficulty for magicians of color. Magic placed them in a position of power and knowledge; but because of its black and white color-coding, also associated them with the forces of darkness. This also helps explain why women could not easily succeed as stage magicians. The unforgotten history of early modern witchcraft panics perpetuated the fear that females who practiced magic would enter into dangerous alliances and acquire

powers that might upset gender hierarchy. This continues to be the case: while professional women conjurers became more common after about 1880, and are by no means unheard of today, they remain a small minority [During, 2002, p. 108].

The result is a paradoxical situation in which supposedly "enlightened" and "rational" audiences in colonizing countries were, through a kind of imperial madness, made irrationally afraid of magicians who were women and people of color. The colonizer's self-aggrandizing affirmation of their own rational superiority is undermined by the anxiety that this superiority is held in bad faith, that it is all a sham.

This contradiction reveals a much-used loophole in the democratizing idea that reason is a universal quality possessed by all humans. Imperial logic does not deny this proposition directly, but gets around its egalitarian consequences by arguing that, while all human beings may contain the *potential* for rational thought, not all cultures have the ability to fulfill it. In the same way that Styers highlights the use by anthropologists of euphemistic terms like "traditional" to describe cultures that were once depicted as "primitive" and "irrational," so too this notion that colonized people are, in a process of seemingly infinite deferral, not *yet* rational plays into a veiled and insidious imperial narrative. This crafty qualification allows the colonizer to conceal base motives such as greed and power by representing their imperial mission as one of enlightened benevolence. The apparent goal is not to exploit the colonized people, but to educate them, to remove the chains of ignorance and irrationality. The colonizer thus disingenuously maintains the self-perception of themselves as "innocent," a subjective position that, as we saw in Chapter 2, is crucial to the perpetuation of a mythology. Clarke replicates this logic of self-serving benevolence in the gentleman with the thistledown hair's constant bullying of Stephen, a form of abuse the gentleman undertakes under the guise of elevating the butler to the position of king. "You intended nothing but kindness, I know," Stephen tells the fairy, as he finally prepares to destroy his former tormentor (Clarke, 2015, p. 983).

Such outwardly munificent aims were little more than a rhetorical veil for the abuses that were undertaken in the name of European imperialism. Both anthropologists and stage magicians were crucial in framing this endeavor in the public mind, and while the contributions of the former group are now well known, the importance of the latter has only

## Chapter 5. Imperialism's Magic Helper

recently begun to be told. One particular object of fascination for both groups, for instance, was the "primitive" magician, whose position at the intersection of social and magical power made them such an important figure, as Jones observes:

> Anthropologists [...] positioned the primitive magician as the ultimate cultural Other against which to test their explanatory prowess as modern social scientists capable of systematically accounting for even the most aberrant (by Enlightenment standards) beliefs and practices in terms of universal laws and generalizable theories. The joint attention they trained on the figure of the primitive magician linked illusionists and anthropologists themselves in another curious relationship of doubleness: illusionists articulated an anthropology of magic while anthropologists quietly absorbed the imagery of illusionism into their ethnographic and theoretical accounts of magic [Jones, 2017, p. 20].

For anthropologists and secular magicians, the "primitive" magician is held up as a useful example of the dangers of irrationality, a move that translates into an implicit justification for colonial rule. Imperial reasoning suggests that it is hardly in the best interests of a "backward" people to be ruled by leaders possessing such unsound logic—indeed, it becomes essentially a moral duty for the colonizer to take charge of such a nation and carve out for it a path toward enlightenment.

During points out that this "educational" mission went beyond the use of churches, schools, and other social institutions to indoctrinate colonized peoples. Stage magicians were also deployed by colonizing powers in an effort to combat the superstitions of the indigenous population, sometimes engaging in open confrontations with local occult magicians. "In the second half of the nineteenth century," writes During, "the British and the French employed various stage conjurers—Jean-Eugène Robert-Houdin (1805–1871), 'Baron' Seeman (1833–1886), and Douglas Beaufort (1864–1939)—to overawe native populations" (During, 2002, p. 10). The underlying racism of these efforts can be seen in the discursive appropriation of the notions of "black" and "white" magic, terms that were not originally racial in origin, but came to be overcoded by reference to skin color:

> European expansion, especially into Africa, perpetuated the old division between "white" magic and pagan or diabolical magics. [...] The old terms "necromancy" (literally, magic conjuring up the dead) and "negromancy" (black or malevolent divination) had been used interchangeably

## English Magic and Imperial Madness

in the medieval period, and the linguistic accident which tied death to blackness would be exploited, perhaps unknowingly, by colonialist discourse. Certainly, after about 1780, African varieties of supernaturalism (often called "mumbo-jumbo," "voodoo," "zombie-ism," and so on) were invoked for a diversity of white agendas [During, 2002, p. 10].

Stage magicians thus not only played a part in framing the imperial endeavor as a benevolent attempt to bring rationality and enlightenment to the colonized population, they were also employed as occasional frontline soldiers in this struggle, using their technical abilities to prove that, through rational skill rather than occult power, they could outdo the local magicians to undermine their "irrational" authority.

The most famous historical example of this kind of confrontational strategy comes from the French illusionist Jean-Eugène Robert-Houdin, arguably the greatest stage magician of his time. One indication of Robert-Houdin's stature in the world of secular magic is that Erik Weisz, a Hungarian immigrant to the United States, later adopted the stage name of Harry Houdini in his honor. Houdini would go on to become one of the greatest illusionists and escape artists of all time, and remains a household name almost a century after his death. Like Norrell, a central part of Robert-Houdin's mission was to make magic respectable to the mainstream of society. In his *Memoirs of Robert-Houdin* (1858), "Robert-Houdin is elevating the secular magician, who had long been thought of as either a vagabond or a charlatan, to middle-class values and ways of life," argues During. "His text thus furnishes new compromises and bridges between being respectable and being in the magic entertainment business" (During, 2002, p. 127). To attain this goal of social respectability, Robert-Houdin deliberately purged his act of all mystification. "Robert-Houdin exemplified an approach to defining his brand of magic as an unambiguously modern combination of skill and expertise, hostile toward any obscurantism and akin to science" (Jones, 2017, p. 7). This was reflected, for instance, in his refusal to wear exotic clothing or wizard's robes, or incorporate occult flourishes into his act. Robert-Houdin's performances were secular magic in its purest, most disenchanted form, adamant in his insistence that no aspect of the supernatural was involved.

One of the most important moments in Robert-Houdin's career is a mission that he undertook to Algeria in 1856. At the time, Algeria was an important French colonial acquisition, and Robert-Houdin was

## Chapter 5. Imperialism's Magic Helper

invited there to use his secular magic to "enlighten" the local people. Robert-Houdin's performances were aimed at a group of indigenous magicians rather than the general public. This assault was strategic, because these magicians held a great deal of political sway among the larger Algerian population. To undermine their authority was thus to strengthen the French imperial cause.

> In 1856, at the behest of the French Army, he traveled to the relatively new colony to stage a series of didactic performances designed to challenge the influence of popular religious figures known as marabouts. According to army intelligence, these marabouts were using magic tricks to convince people that they were anointed with supernatural powers, and then leading their awestruck followers in messianic, anticolonial campaigns. Robert-Houdin's mission was to one-up the marabouts with technologically advanced trickery, and to ultimately discredit them as charlatans among Algerian Muslims [Jones, 2017, p. 12].

Robert-Houdin's battle with the Algerian magicians was "both literal and allegorical" (Jones, 2017, p. 14), an event in which he imagined himself as a force for rational good over the deceitful and irrational marabouts. Whatever the "enlightened" and "heroic" measures that Robert-Houdin used to interpret his own actions, the truth is that they were deployed in a racist and oppressive cause. "Robert-Houdin's mission is an extraordinary example of the use of spectacle in European imperialist projects to astound, frighten, and/or beguile indigenous spectators and dramatize knowledge differentials, enacting and reinforcing assumptions about the superiority of European civilization," contends Jones. "Europeans' production of such imperialist performances went hand-in-hand with the consumption of Orientalist images of North African Muslims as irrational, childish fanatics" (Jones, 2017, p. 39). Although Robert-Houdin's stated intention was an act "crusading against primitive unreason" (Jones, 2017, p. 74), in reality he only succeeds in flaunting France's imperial dominance.

## *The Magic Helper*

The rise of postcolonial criticism in recent decades was preceded in the twentieth century by the work of the Frankfurt School of Critical Theory that, in its analysis of the connection between rationality and power, also provided the basis for a powerful rethinking of the relationship between magic and imperialism. The Frankfurt School thinkers were particularly distressed by the concurrence of Enlightenment rationality and totalitarian politics, exemplified by the rise of Nazism in Germany. In his book *Escape from Freedom* (1941), for instance, Erich Fromm sets out to determine how it is possible for these two antagonistic ways of approaching the world to coexist in a disenchanted world. Fromm's analysis rests on an important distinction between external freedom, such as democratic rights or economic well-being, and inner freedom, by which he means the psychological sense of who we are as human beings. If the inner sense of freedom is inadequately developed, making a person psychologically reliant on an authority figure, this emotional need can potentially overpower the preservation of external freedom, resulting in totalitarianism.

Drawing on the work of the German psychoanalyst Karen Horney, Fromm explains that humans pass through a stage of immaturity in which they attach themselves to what Fromm calls a "magic helper." A "magic helper" can take on many forms, from God to a parental figure, but the specific manifestation is not important. What matters is how the immature person passes through a phase of idealization and worship of this "magic helper," submitting wholeheartedly to the authority of their idol. "Frequently, of course, the 'magic helper' is personified: he is conceived of as God, as a principle, or as real persons such as one's parent, husband, wife, or superior," writes Fromm. "It is important to recognize that when real persons assume the role of the magic helper they are endowed with magic qualities, and the significance they have results from their being the personification of the magic helper" (Fromm, 1994, p. 173). This formative experience can initiate a psychological pattern in which a person unconsciously seeks to replicate this relationship with the "magic helper":

> This process of personification of the magic helper is to be observed frequently in what is called "falling in love." A person with that kind of relatedness to the magic helper seeks to find him in flesh and blood. For some reason or other—often supported by sexual desires—a certain other person assumes for him those magic qualities, and he makes that person into the being to whom and on whom his whole life becomes related and dependent. The fact that the other person frequently does the same with the first one does not alter the picture. It only helps to strengthen the impression that this relationship is one of "real love" [Fromm, 1994, p. 173].

## Chapter 5. Imperialism's Magic Helper

The proper resolution of this stage occurs when the "person who is dependent on the magic helper also feels, although often unconsciously, enslaved by 'him' and, to a greater or lesser degree, rebels against 'him'" (Fromm, 1994, p. 175). Rebellion against the "magic helper" leads to a burgeoning sense of autonomy and individuality—the onset, in other words, of maturity. The problem with modern society, for Fromm, is that too often it infantilizes its subjects. A human being may thus have all the markers of external freedom—a political consciousness, a family life, a steady job—but remain psychologically attached to the authority of the "magic helper." Fromm concludes that this condition is what makes modern society vulnerable to totalitarian forms of government.

Another important response from the Frankfurt School is Theodor Adorno and Max Horkheimer's *Dialectic of Enlightenment* (1944), a book that was composed while its authors were living in exile in the United States, having fled the threat of Nazism in Germany. As a result, they, like Fromm, examine some urgent questions about the coexistence of rationality and totalitarianism. Adorno and Horkheimer's definition of enlightenment goes far beyond its usual historical limits, referring instead to the rise of a philosophical rationalism that they detect as already present in ancient Greek culture—indeed, the heroic figure of Odysseus, with his reputation for cunning, is singled out as an early prototype of the enlightened human being. Adorno and Horkheimer's account draws unconsciously from Weber's disenchantment narrative. They repeat the idea, for instance, that the rise of rationality has made "primitive" ways of thinking impossible because they are grounded in magic: "Both reason and religion outlaw the principle of magic" (Adorno & Horkheimer, 2002, p. 13). Instead, the new laws of enlightened rationality reshape not only humanity's relationship to the world around it, but also its conception of power.

Adorno and Horkheimer's do not, however, regard the advent of enlightened rationality as an inherently positive step in human history. They argue instead that enlightened logic makes abstraction the primary perspective through which the world is viewed. This abstract framework reduces the particularity of human experience to a generalized logical category. Adorno and Horkheimer argue that this philosophical mode of abstraction makes possible, in turn, an imperial mode of politics. "The distance of subject from object, the presupposition of abstraction, is founded on the distance from things which the ruler attains by means of the ruled," they write. "The songs of Homer and the hymns of the *Rig Veda* date from the time of territorial dominion and its strongholds, when a warlike race of overlords imposed itself on the defeated indigenous population" (Adorno & Horkheimer, 2002, p. 9). In short, while rationality may indeed be capable of empowering a small minority of people, for Adorno and Horkheimer, history has repeatedly proven that such selective liberation only leads to the oppression of others. The example of Robert-Houdin is a case in point: his confrontation with the Algerian magicians may have been carried out in the name of enlightened rationality, but his underlying intention was always to dominate rather than empower them.

There is no attempt in *Dialectic of Enlightenment* to romanticize the pre–Enlightenment world, however. Magical thinking had no abstract conception of a unified nature, argue Adorno and Horkheimer, but instead regarded the world as a radical particularity:

> The spirit which practiced magic was not single or identical; it changed with the cult masks which represented the multiplicity of spirits. Magic is bloody untruth, but in it domination is not yet disclaimed by transforming itself into a pure truth underlying the world which it enslaves. [...] It is the identity of mind and its correlative, the unity of nature, which subdues the abundance of qualities. Nature, stripped of qualities, becomes the chaotic stuff of mere classification, and the all-powerful self becomes a mere having, an abstract identity. Magic implies specific representation [Adorno & Horkheimer, 2002, p. 6].

Without rational abstraction, the objects and practices involved in ritual sacrifices and magical practices were not being inflicted on easily-replaceable symbolic doubles. "What is done to the spear, the hair, the name of the enemy, is also to befall his person; the sacrificial animal is slain in place of the god" (Adorno & Horkheimer, 2002, p. 6). There are violence and oppression in the world of magic that Adorno and Horkheimer describe, but there is also a respect for the divine order that values in life "the sanctity of the *hic et nunc*" (Adorno & Horkheimer, 2002, p. 6) that disappears after humanity exits from this state.

Some of the most memorable examples given of this transition in *Dialectic of Enlightenment* involve Odysseus, the prototypical enlightenment rationalist, breaking the contracts of the ancient order. He does so not by defying these conventions directly, but by discovering logical loopholes that allow him to benefit without paying the expected

## Chapter 5. Imperialism's Magic Helper

price—having himself tied to the mast to hear the forbidden song of the sirens, for instance, or referring to himself as "Nobody" in order to escape revenge from the blinded cyclops Polyphemus. Odysseus's skill at overcoming such obstacles demonstrates how this form of rationality can be used as a means of empowerment. Yet while Odysseus avoids paying what he owes by using his cunning, Adorno and Horkheimer contend that enlightened rationality requires of humanity a different, more insidious price. Pre-enlightenment religion instilled a holy fear of the gods, but it also provided comfort in knowing that human fate was in the hands of the divine magical helpers. There is no such reassurance for modern humanity, argue Adorno and Horkheimer, which is plagued by a constant sense of anxiety:

> The gods cannot take away fear from human beings, the petrified cries of whom they bear as their names. Humans believe themselves free of fear when there is no longer anything unknown. This has determined the path of demythologization, of enlightenment, which equates the living with the nonliving as myth had equated the nonliving with the living. Enlightenment is mythical fear radicalized. The pure immanence of positivism, its ultimate product, is nothing other than a form of universal taboo. Nothing is allowed to remain outside, since the mere idea of the "outside" is the real source of fear [Adorno & Horkheimer, 2002, p. 11].

Reason can provide no respite from this anxiety, but instead transforms itself, Adorno and Horkheimer contend, into "mythical fear" (Adorno & Horkheimer, 2002, p. 11). Enlightenment is unable to extricate itself from myths of power because the irrationality of the latter always takes precedence. That is why, in a memorable line from their 1944 preface to *Dialectic of Enlightenment*, Adorno and Horkheimer conclude that "enlightenment reverts to mythology" (Adorno & Horkheimer, 2002, p. xviii).

The world of magic and sacrifice that Adorno and Horkheimer portray in their book is often filled with darkness and anxiety. The magic helpers of the ancients, the gods, are often cruel and arbitrary. There is no sense in *Dialectic of Enlightenment* that a return to this way of life is desirable, or even possible. The underlying purpose of Adorno and Horkheimer's analysis is to show that enlightened rationality is a false alternative, providing only a mirage of empowerment that comes at the price of reason itself. "The history of civilization is the history of the introversion of sacrifice—in other words, the history of renunciation," they write. "All who renounce give away more of their life than is given back to them, more than the life they preserve" (Adorno & Horkheimer, 2002, p. 43). The "antireason of totalitarian capitalism" (Adorno & Horkheimer, 2002, p. 43) derives from the enlightened subject making a bargain in which they lose far more than they gain, but which is nonetheless presented to them psychologically, mythically, as a benefit. In other words, enlightened rationality is driving modern society mad, and it has perversely accepted this fate in the name of reason:

> This very denial, the core of all civilizing rationality, is the germ cell of proliferating mythical irrationality: with the denial of nature in human beings, not only the *telos* of the external mastery of nature but also the *telos* of one's own life becomes confused and opaque. At the moment when human beings cut themselves off from the consciousness of themselves as nature, all the purposes for which they keep themselves alive—social progress, the heightening of material and intellectual forces, indeed, consciousness itself—become void, and the enthronement of the means as the end, which in late capitalism is taking on the character of overt madness, is already detectable in the earliest history of subjectivity [Adorno & Horkheimer, 2002, pp. 42–43].

Adorno and Horkheimer thus excoriate the false promise of enlightened rationality, which presents itself as a logic of empowerment and freedom. Its claim to have eliminated myth through the power of reason, it turns out, was itself a myth, and the eventual result was "overt madness" and "antireason" (Adorno & Horkheimer, 2002, p. 43). There are few things more dangerous than a madness that continues to believe that it is fundamentally, inherently rational.

The criticisms presented by Fromm and Adorno and Horkheimer provide an important counter-narrative to the imperial mindset that historically has pervaded the discourse about magic. In particular, they do much to expose and refute the racism and oppression that has underpinned the putative rationality of modern society. Nonetheless, the weak point of their analysis lies in the fact that, despite this critique of rationality, they continue to maintain an ongoing belief in the power of reason. Josephson-Storm articulates this problem particularly well when he writes that *Dialectic of Enlightenment*

> is effectively a late expression of an old myth. It rests on a set of basically mythical binaries (myth/enlightenment, nature/human) whose breaches it stages, but nevertheless maintains. [...] [I]t works by granting the

## Chapter 5. Imperialism's Magic Helper

triumph of disenchantment and de-animation even as it traces the negative impacts of this process and its potential returns in new myth. But this assertion of loss relies on the assumption that reason once ruled or turned into its opposite. Yet, this event never occurred. It too is a myth [Josephson-Storm, 2017, p. 10].

The Frankfurt School thinkers thus provide a powerful critique of modern reason, but this endeavor is weakened by their implication that reason itself remains the solution to this problem. "The neurotic person is the one who has not given up fighting against complete submission, but who, at the same time, has remained bound to the figure of the magic helper, whatever form or shape 'he' may have assumed," writes Fromm in *Escape from Reason*. "His neurosis is always to be understood as an attempt, and essentially an unsuccessful one, to solve the conflict between that basic dependency and the quest for freedom" (Fromm, 1994, p. 177). Fromm yearns for this neurotic subject to free himself from his dependence on a "magic helper" and emerge into psychological independence, thus ensuring a rational, stable existence. The Frankfurt School thinkers mourn for a reason that has been misused and appropriated by power, leading them to fantasize about a purer, untainted reason that is redeployed ethically. "If what you are doing in the mode of enlightenment critique is lamenting the disillusion of myth, then myth has not been dissolved," responds Josephson-Storm. "Your mourning reinstates the object of your grief" (Josephson-Storm, 2017, p. 10). Reason, in short, cannot be the answer, because it cannot be made ethical by detaching it from the realm of power and politics—that, too, is another form of myth.

The solution lies instead in a critical unreason, an unreason that is not reason's opposite, but its mirror image, its fictional double. It is within this parallel space of literary unreason that humanity is able to take a break from the demands of reason, to have the freedom to play with what is normally serious, in order to test the true urgency of reason's claims. Clarke is undertaking just such an experiment in the pages of *Jonathan Strange and Mr. Norrell*, providing the reader with a provocatively mythologized double of England's imperial history. It is possible, of course, that readers may read the novel uncritically, choosing to regard Norrell and Strange as their own "magic helpers." Indeed, in Chapter 36, Strange compares the job of a magician to that of a colonial explorer heading off to survey the rivers of Africa. When Arabella exclaims that she assumed he was a magician rather than an explorer, Strange replies that the two occupations are not all that different from each other. Just as a true explorer must go beyond the reading of maps and venture out of the house into the larger world, he tells Arabella, so too magicians must go beyond the books in their library to engage in actual magic (Clarke, 2015, pp. 507–508). A more judicious reading of the novel suggests that by the end of the novel the reader ought to have wearied of Strange and Norrell, these "magic helpers" whose shortcomings are so starkly revealed in the course of the narrative. If enlightenment always reverts to myth, as Adorno and Horkheimer claim, then Clarke's novel provides an artificial myth, a fragment of unreason through which we may get a glimpse of reason from the other side.

## Chapter 6

# The Reason of Unreason

## *Magic and Madness*

It is conventional to think of reason and madness as existing in simple opposition to each other, even though the line between the rational and the irrational, in practice, can never be truly delineated. For these two categories are always entangled in complex and hybrid ways, each reflecting on and defining the other. In his study *Madness in Civilization* (2015), for instance, Andrew Scull portrays madness as a specter that haunts humanity's aspirations to logical rigor by slipping constantly outside the comprehension of medicine and science:

> Madness extends beyond the medical grasp in other ways. It remains a source of recurrent fascination for writers and artists, and for their audiences. Novels, biographies, autobiographies, plays, films, paintings, sculpture—in all these realms and more, Unreason continues to haunt the imagination and to surface in powerful and unpredictable ways. All attempts to corral and contain it, to reduce it to some single essence seem doomed to disappointment [Scull, 2015, p. 15].

For a more nuanced approach to an understanding of madness, then, it is necessary to abandon the problematic idea of insanity as a "single essence," and instead conceive of rationality and irrationality as interdependent categories, the meaning of which we can only glimpse when we regard them as mutually defining.

This way of thinking is suggested from the outset by the title of *Jonathan Strange and Mr. Norrell*, which implicitly invites the reader to compare and contrast its eponymous characters. The Raven King's prophecy, as recited by Vinculus, specifies that there must be *two* magicians, for instance, although it is hard to imagine a more poorly matched pair than Strange and Norrell. Norrell is dry and rational, a scholar who lacks social graces, hungers for political power, and aims

## English Magic and Imperial Madness

to transform magic from its current lowly position into the pursuit of respectable gentlemen. However, when Norrell first enters the London social scene as England's only practical magician, these aspects of his character are not widely known. As such, Norrell is initially taken by the public, wrongly, to be a madman, the latest iteration in a long line of unhinged street performers claiming to be the Raven King (Clarke, 2015, p. 22). While this first impression turns out to be baseless, Norrell is the exception, at least among magicians, that proves the rule. The centrality of madness to the practice of magic is reiterated, for instance, in this exchange from Clarke's short story "The Ladies of Grace Adieu":

> "Strange," said Henry Woodhope, "you are quite as ridiculous as ever."
> "Do not mind him, Henry," said Arabella Strange. "He has the mind of a magician. They are all a little mad."
> "Except Norrell," said Strange [Clarke, 2007b, p. 16].

It is Strange, naturally, who provides the bright, romantic counterpart to Norrell's dull rationalism, setting in motion an interplay between magic and reason that constitutes one of the book's most important themes.

The proximity of magic to madness is restated continually in the course of *Jonathan Strange and Mr. Norrell*. Consider, for instance, how Starecross Hall, which Segundus and Honeyfoot initially intended to renovate and turn into a school for magicians, is repurposed as a home for the insane after Norrell blocks their original plans. Childermass observes drily that the house would serve equally well as a refuge for the mad and as a school for magicians, implying that these two conditions share a commensurate way of thinking (Clarke, 2015, p. 591). Indeed, madness is so closely tied to what makes magic possible that the latter cannot be used to cure the former, as Strange discovers when he attempts to find a remedy for the madness of King George III. Looking through the extensive collection of books in Norrell's library, Strange is astonished to find that almost no spells exist for the cure of insanity (Clarke, 2015, p. 447). When Strange confers with Norrell on the matter a few pages later, the latter is unsurprised by his protégé's lack of success. The Aureate magicians, he points out, were unable to cure madness—indeed, they often seemed to celebrate this condition, believing that madmen possessed secret knowledge that could enhance the practice of magic, so that famous magicians like Ralph Stokesey and Catherine of Winchester were known to consult with the insane. Strange draws

## Chapter 6. The Reason of Unreason

Norrell's attention to the fact that fairies, too, are often drawn to madness in their human counterparts, with Norrell confirming that much had been written about the resemblance between fairies and the insane (Clarke, 2015, p. 466). Magic cannot drive out madness, in Clarke's novel, because magic itself constitutes a form of madness. The divergent methods of Strange and Norrell represent two different responses to this problem, with Strange seeking to push unreason to its limits, while Norrell, by contrast, aims to formulate a magic that operates within the limits of reason alone.

Clarke also provides the reader with a non-human perspective in the form of the gentleman with the thistledown hair. Even though fairies are the traditional source of English magic, their erratic and devious tendencies are seen by Norrell, in particular, as something to be feared and suppressed. In short, fairies do not represent the kind of "respectable" magic that Norrell wants to promote in his restoration of English magic. Clarke reveals the hypocrisy of Norrell's position when he summons the gentleman with the thistledown hair to resurrect Lady Pole. Because of his in-depth knowledge of the history of English magic, Norrell nonetheless turns out to be the novel's most valuable source of information about fairies, as shown in his lengthy discussions with Strange on this topic. In one such disquisition, for instance, Norrell reiterates the peculiar affinity between fairies and madmen by telling the story of a lunatic from Bristol who became the devoted friend of one of his dining chairs. By any human standard, the man was insane, but the fairies, recounts Norrell, had quite a different view of the situation:

> Clearly the man was mad, but Chaston says that fairies would not consider his behaviour as ridiculous as we do. Fairies do not make a strong distinction between the animate and the inanimate. They believe that stones, doors, trees, fire, clouds and so forth all have souls and desires, and are either masculine or feminine. Perhaps this explains the extraordinary sympathy for madness which fairies exhibit [Clarke, 2015, p. 466].

In an earlier footnote, Clarke cites this same (fictional) scholar to show how the affinity between fairies and madness is the precondition for their magical aptitude: "Chaston wrote that men and fairies both contain within them a faculty of reason and a faculty of magic. In men reason is strong and magic is weak. With fairies it is the other way round: magic comes very naturally to them, but by human standards they are barely sane" (Clarke, 2015, p. 299). Clues such as these are scattered throughout *Jonathan Strange and Mr. Norrell*, and it is by examining them judiciously that the careful reader can deduce the connection Clarke is drawing between magic and madness.

## *Reason's Double*

Clarke is guarded when, in a BBC interview, she is asked about what inspired the creation of her characters. "Strange has a touch of Byron in him, I suppose, and a little of the eighteenth-century rakes—Valmont in *Les Liaisons Dangereuses* and so forth," she responds (Clarke, 2004). The Raven King was derived, in part, from the Gray Mage of Paln in Ursula Le Guin's *Earthsea* trilogy and the Mouth of Sauron, a magician who appears near the end of *The Lord of the Rings*, reveals Clarke, while Norrell is based on a combination of Clarke herself and "a really great jigsaw with a picture of a huge library and two or three old gentlemen with eighteenth-century wigs reading books" (Clarke, 2004). Yet the seemingly crucial opposition between Strange and Norrell is often brought into question in the course of the novel. Consider, for instance, Strange's complaint, while assisting the British army in Portugal, that the military cannot tell the difference between the two magicians. He grumbles that the soldiers refer to him arbitrarily as either Strange or Norrell, and seem to have no idea that they are two different people (Clarke, 2015, p. 379). For all the ostensible differences separating the two magicians, the novel encourages the reader to see them as overlapping figures, simultaneously attracting and repelling one another, symbiotic doubles that rely on each other for their mutual definition.

This logic of doubling extends, in particular, to those characters who are portrayed as being under the influence of magic, a condition that manifests itself, in the non-magical world, as madness: indeed, Clarke blurs the lines between these two states so masterfully that it is impossible to distinguish between them. The gentleman with the thistledown hair exchanges Arabella Strange for an animated piece of moss-oak shaped in her image, for instance, with the fairy using this uncanny likeness to trick Strange into giving up his wife. Stephen is likewise able to fulfill his duties as a servant while undertaking magical adventures using a similar mode of substitution. Lady Pole's is the

## Chapter 6. The Reason of Unreason

novel's most complicated duplication, so that when Childermass visits her at Starecross Hall, only his sensitivity to magic allows him to detect her divided existence. When Childermass looks at Lady Pole, he is literally seeing double, two women instead of one, as though she were reflected in a mirror, except that she somehow seems to be in two places at once. This impression turns out to be correct: Lady Pole really is in two places at the same time, with one version of herself sitting in a chair at Starecross Hall, calm and wearing a white dress, while the other version, furious and sporting a red dress, is trapped in the mad world of Faerie. Even when she speaks to Childermass, her voice comes to him in stereo (Clarke, 2015, p. 934). The duality of reason and madness becomes especially evident at this moment, with the reasonable version of Lady Pole, trapped in Fairie, drowned out by the nonsensical story she recounts in Starecross Hall. As such, the two voices contradict and clash with each other, the more powerful narrative of the madwoman's story obscuring what is being said by the Lady Pole trapped in Faerie (Clarke, 2015, pp. 934–935). The split between the two Lady Poles is resolved shortly afterward when the severed little finger, which the fairy took as a token of her enchantment, is restored: "The finger flowed into the hand, making a seamless whole. In the same instant the impression of endless, dreary corridors surrounding them disappeared; the two women before Childermass's eyes resolved themselves into one" (Clarke, 2015, p. 936). Rather than entering a world of utter nonsense, the insane dimension of the magical realm in these examples entails a twisted version of rationality, a logic that, by turning in on itself, becomes the perverse double of reason rather than abolishing it altogether.

A similar notion of madness is central to Foucault's landmark 1961 work on the history of the asylum, translated into English in abridged form as *Madness and Civilization: A History of Madness in the Age of Reason* and, more recently, in a complete version as *History of Madness*. In a 1982 interview with Rux Martin, Foucault explains that his motivation for studying insanity grew out of his own paradoxical interests and desires:

> Each of my works is a part of my own biography. For one or another reason I had the occasion to feel and live those things. To take a simple example, I used to work in a psychiatric hospital in the 1950s. After having studied philosophy, I wanted to see what madness was: I had been mad enough to study reason; I was reasonable enough to study madness [Martin, 1988, p. 11].

## English Magic and Imperial Madness

Foucault characterizes his method as one of approaching his chosen topic from the opposite side to which it is conventionally viewed—he begins, in other words, with its peripheral double, and proceeds to work his way back to the center of a discourse. This technique is more clearly visible in the original French title of Foucault's text, *Folie et déraison: Histoire de la folie à l'âge classique*, which brings together the usual French word for madness (*folie*) and pairs it with the unconventional term *déraison*, translated into English as "unreason" (it would be obscured once again when, in the second French edition of 1972, Foucault dropped the original title in favor of the subtitle).

In his foreword to the new translation of *History of Madness*, Ian Hacking draws the reader's attention to this concept of "unreason," so boldly emphasized in the original text and yet which becomes, as time goes by, "a bit like Alice's Cheshire Cat, of which nothing is left but the grin" (Hacking, 2006, p. ix). "What is the *déraison* that dropped from the title but was still all over the text?" asks Hacking. "Unreason is not identical to madness but something that contrasts with it" (Hacking, 2006, p. x). There are various reasons for Foucault's changing perspective on this term—his acrimonious debate with Derrida over how to interpret the connection between madness and Descartes's concept of the Cogito, for instance, or the new emphasis on Nietzschean genealogy that marks Foucault's work of the 1970s—but Hacking insists that the concept, for all its ambivalence, remains a key idea in *History of Madness*. Its necessity stems from a philosophical break with Greek thought that arises in the medieval period for, Foucault points out in the 1961 preface, "the Greek Logos had no opposite. European man, since the depths of the Middle Ages, has had a relation to a thing that is confusedly termed Madness, Dementia or Unreason. It is perhaps to that obscure presence that Western Reason owes something of its depth" (Foucault, 2006, p. xxix). Greenwood contends in *The Anthropology of Magic* that this lacuna in Greek thought also had important consequences for the history of magic:

> Today, myth is often considered to be fictitious because it is associated with magic, but the early Greeks highly valued the poetic discourse of *mythos*. [...] It was only later that *mythos* became opposed to *logos*, and *logos* became privileged. *Logos* is Greek for "word, speech, discourse," and also "reason" and the use of rational and logical argument. As a word, *myth* only came into the English language during the nineteenth century,

## Chapter 6. The Reason of Unreason

and at this time, it already had the negative connotations accorded to it from classical Greece, where it referred to a nonrational, or even deceptive, set of ideas or false consciousness[.] [...] The purpose of *logos* was to establish truth on the basis of the so-called laws of thought and thus through logical, critical and detached intelligence alone. Everything earlier attributed to speech as the power to impress and convince was reduced to *mythos*, "the stuff of the fabulous, the marvelous" [Greenwood, 2009, pp. 76–77].

The shift that both Foucault and Greenwood identify does not derive from the creation of an entirely new concept—the Greeks did not lack the idea of madness, after all—but arises from the growing habit of regarding such terms as magic and science, or reason and madness, as interlocking notions that are theoretically opposed to one another.

The most powerful subversion of the supposed "naturalness" of this dichotomy comes from the observation that historically, in many cultures, these ideas and practices lived side-by-side without conflict or even, in some cases, any clear distinction. Judging the difference between magic and religion, for instance, is a constant problem for historians of magic, as Thomas points out in *Religion and the Decline of Magic*. Thomas observes, for instance, how the rituals of the medieval church, when presented to an uneducated public, helped to blur the lines between the two categories: "The medieval Church [...] did a great deal to weaken the fundamental distinction between a prayer and a charm, and to encourage the idea that there was virtue in the mere repetition of holy words" (Thomas, 2003, p. 47). In *History of Madness*, Foucault contends that the reception of madness follows a similar trajectory. The medieval societies of Europe integrated the insane into the structures of everyday life. The emerging concept of "unreason," by contrast, increasingly relegated them to a position outside, or in opposition to, the newly established boundaries of the society of reason.

The result of this separation, for Foucault, was that it ended the ongoing cultural dialogue between madness and sanity. As such, the great political dream of modernity evolved into one of social purity, of a reason purged of its shadowy double. The eventual result was the establishment, in the eighteenth century, of the discipline of psychiatry, which Foucault characterizes in his 1961 preface as "a monologue by reason *about* madness" (Foucault, 2006, p. xxviii), a one-sided discourse in which the mad have no stake. In Chapter III of *History of Madness*,

## English Magic and Imperial Madness

Foucault demonstrates the effects of this new logic on the understanding of magic by examining a 1682 French edict suppressing "all those who describe themselves as soothsayers, magicians and enchanters" (Foucault, 2006, p. 95). Whereas such laws previously aimed to punish magic as an affront to religion or morality, this edict instead argues that magicians should be prosecuted on the grounds of fraudulence. As a result,

> magic is stripped of the efficacious power of sacrilege: it is no longer profanation, but is reduced instead to mere trickery. Its power is illusion, both in the sense that it is devoid of reality and in that it blinds the weak-willed and the feeble-minded. If it still belonged to the realm of evil, it was no longer due to the manner in which its action demonstrated dark transcendent powers, but because it took its place in a system of errors that had its dupes and artisans, its illusionists and its gullible public. Witchcraft was on occasion the vehicle for real crimes, but in itself it was no longer a criminal gesture or a sacrilegious action. Severed from its sacred power, it became little more than a vector for malicious intent, an illusion of the mind at the service of unquiet hearts. It was no longer judged according to its profanatory illusions, but according to what unreason it revealed [Foucault, 2006, p. 95].

Foucault thus locates a conceptual point where madness and magic converge in the disenchanted modern world. The association that is forged between these two categories rests on their shared connection to the rise of "unreason," an opposition that, as Foucault demonstrates, is inherently political in its origins.

The notion of insanity as reason's double actually precedes the early modern idea of unreason, as the *History of Madness* demonstrates by detailing a series of literary metaphors, from Sebastian Brant's *Ship of Fools* (1494) to Erasmus's *Praise of Folly* (1511), in which the everyday world is pointedly emulated by the insane. Foucault detects in these symbolic doubles a fruitful dialogue between reason and madness. Crucial to this interchange is the awareness, rooted in a Christian consciousness of human sinfulness, that intellectual pride can be a subtle trap that may delude even the most sophisticated person into believing, erroneously, that they are wise. As such, Erasmus self-consciously deploys his text as a kind of "mirror" that playfully reveals the reader's self-deceptions by reversing the values of conventional wisdom. Erasmus's character Folly thus proclaims: "Anyone who argued that I was Minerva or Wisdom

## Chapter 6. The Reason of Unreason

could easily be convinced of his mistake simply by the sight of me, even if I never spoke a word, though speech is the least deceptive mirror of the mind" (Erasmus, 1993, p. 13). Commenting on the importance of Erasmus's work in *History of Madness*, Foucault writes:

> In this imaginary adhesion to the self, madness is born like a mirage. From now on, the symbol of madness was to be a mirror, which reflected nothing real, but secretly showed the presumptuous dreams of all who gazed into it to contemplate themselves. Madness here was not about truth or the world, but rather about man and the truth about himself that he can perceive [Foucault, 2006, p. 24].

In Erasmus's paradigm, the symbolic role of the mad, effectively, is to provide a measure of everyday sanity, a crucial mirror in which we can detect the delusions created by our intellectual pride. As such, the insane are still perceived as a necessary component of a critical dialogue about who we are and what we believe.

A philosophical shift occurs in the seventeenth century that changes the terms of this interaction. Whereas for Erasmus the *inclusion* of the mad played a crucial part in determining the true limits of reason, Foucault points to Descartes, in particular his formulation of the Cogito in *Discourse on Method* (1637), as the beginning of a paradigm in which reason is defined instead by the radical *exclusion* of madness. Angelos Evangelou explains this new configuration in *Philosophizing Madness from Nietzsche to Derrida* (2017):

> Unreason, therefore, is what reason made of madness, or it is what madness becomes after the labelling of madness by reason as its absolute opposite. This is an act with a double effect in the sense that by excluding madness as its opposite, reason simultaneously establishes itself as what it is. In other words, the exclusion of madness is constitutive of reason itself [Evangelou, 2017, p. 143].

Madness remains reason's double after this shift, but only in a disavowed sense. Whereas insanity once had a positive role in defining the boundaries of reason, now it only has a negative function, silencing the voice of madness and reducing rationality to the "monologue" identified by Foucault in the 1961 preface. The original stated intention of Foucault's book was to end this silence, to give a new voice to madness, freeing it from the intellectual arrogance, as Erasmus would have seen it, of a tyrannical reason incapable of admitting its limitations.

## English Magic and Imperial Madness

This objective would result in one of the most bitter intellectual disagreements in modern French philosophy when, in 1963, Derrida delivered a paper titled "Cogito and the History of Madness," in which he drew particular attention to Foucault's reading of Descartes. In contrast to Foucault's claim that Descartes arbitrarily dismisses the possibility of madness in the Cogito, Derrida argues that Descartes's contemplation of the possibility that an evil demon is misleading him should be regarded as the Cogito's formative engagement with madness. Slavoj Žižek summarizes what is at stake in this debate:

> Foucault and Derrida's polemic is one in which they share the key underlying premise: that *Cogito* is inherently related to madness. The difference is that for Foucault, *Cogito* is grounded in the exclusion of madness, while, for Derrida, *Cogito* itself can only emerge through a "mad" hyperbole (universalized doubt), and remains marked by this excess [Žižek, 2014, p. 28].

Foucault defended his position fiercely, penning a scintillating response to Derrida in the 1972 preface to the second edition of his book. Nonetheless, there are signs that Derrida's critique forced Foucault to rethink his position in various ways, even as the latter refused to accept its validity—the change of the book's title, for instance, and the demotion, as Hacking notes, of the once-central notion of "unreason."

The most problematic aspect of Foucault's project lies in his stated goal of breaking the silence of madness, which risks replicating the shortcomings of the psychologist. Is it not likely that Foucault, in trying to give voice to the insane, would simply end up once again imposing the tyranny of reason on them? This point is made by Felman in the opening chapter of *Writing and Madness*, in which she reexamines the Foucault/Derrida debate from the perspective of a literary critic. How is it possible, she ponders, to speak from inside madness, as Foucault aimed to do, rather than about it, from the outside?

> What does it mean, then, to *talk about madness!* Since the publication of Michel Foucault's provocative *History of Madness*, many French intellectuals have repeated Foucault's claim: madness is, primarily, a lack of language, an "absence of production," the silence of a stifled, repressed language. Accordingly, our historic task would be to give madness a voice, to restore its language: a language *of* madness and not *about* it. Now, our present cultural predicament, in Foucault's view, derives precisely from our incapacity to articulate this language: while intending to

## Chapter 6. The Reason of Unreason

"say madness," one is necessarily constrained to speak *about* it [Felman, 2003, p. 14].

In Felman's analysis, neither Foucault nor Derrida is able to provide a satisfactory answer to this problem while remaining in the rational domain of philosophy. As such, the circuitous solution to this quandary delivered by each thinker involves a diversion of philosophy through the language of literature:

> Derrida and Foucault thereby agree on the existence of a literary buffer zone between madness and thought. This literary zone does not, however, play for each the same role, in relation to philosophy. For Foucault, literature gives evidence *against* philosophy; this is not the case for Derrida. For Foucault, the fictions of madness undermine, *disorient* thought. For Derrida, on the contrary, at least in the case of Descartes, the fiction of madness has as its end to *orient* philosophy [Felman, 2003, p. 48].

As such, "the communication between thought and madness cannot be direct, but necessarily must pass through fiction" (Felman, 2003, p. 50)—in other words, literature functions as the fictional double of philosophical reason. Fiction is the magical transformation of that reason, not into madness as such, but into a kind of unreason, a Wonderland into which reason can temporarily escape from itself in order to regain its bearings.

This philosophical discussion of insanity provides a powerful tool for understanding and interpreting *Jonathan Strange and Mr. Norrell*, a work of literature that similarly takes madness (and magic, its close associate in the discourse of unreason) as one of its central themes. At the same time, there is a sense in which *History of Madness*, for all its sophisticated analysis, does not really move all that far beyond the ethical critique offered by Erasmus. After all, Foucault's real purpose may be seen as the act of holding up a mirror to the intellectual arrogance and tyranny of modern reason. The true reclamation of insanity does not lie in Foucault's original aim of allowing madness to speak, therefore, but in the rediscovery of unreason as a necessary limitation on the tyrannical powers of reason. Works like *Jonathan Strange and Mr. Norrell*, which follow in the spirit of this endeavor, ought to be regarded, in turn, as literary mirrors, generating reason's doubles not for the sake of speaking insanity, but in order to rediscover, through fiction, the hidden reason of unreason.

## Reason and Unreason

The hidden reason of unreason sounds like an oxymoron, but it simply connotes that the discourse of insanity is not *pure* nonsense. There is, in other words, a method underlying madness, as Polonius famously observes of Hamlet, even if that logic does not follow the conventional paths of reason. The difficulty that the modern subject faces in confronting this hidden reason arises primarily from the cultural expectations created by the Cartesian revolution. The Cartesian subject allows no place for madness, since this aspect of human experience has been banished from the domain of rationality: quite simply, at a theoretical level, the existence of this hidden reason cannot (and must not) be admitted. Nonetheless, the reality of its disavowed power and attraction is attested to by the fascination exerted, in the realm of fiction, by tales of madness and magic, by the undeniable pull of the putatively irrational on people who would otherwise be considered rational subjects.

This attraction should not be mistaken for a romantic penchant: rather, it is a crucial regulatory mechanism that Foucault identifies in the *Introduction to Kant's Anthropology from a Pragmatic Point of View*, a text completed in 1961 alongside *History of Madness* as part of his doctoral degree, but not published until 2003. John Iliopoulos provides an extensive commentary on this work in the opening chapter of *The History of Reason in the Age of Madness* (2017), arguing that Kant's distinction in the original *Anthropology from a Pragmatic Point of View* (1798) between rationality and reason is a crucial idea that informed Foucault's approach when writing *History of Madness*:

> Reason is transformed into a form of rationality when it ceases to be regulatory and becomes a principle of knowledge when it abandons its transcendental domain in order to become empirical. Reason has no end other than itself; therefore, when it is forced to pursue ends foreign to reflection and speculation, it necessarily generates illusions. Reason is sacrificed the moment it is turned into a principle. This is how rationality is born [Iliopoulos, 2017, p. 8].

In choosing Kant as his primary source, Foucault emphasizes that his critique of modern rationality proceeds from the very heart of Enlightenment reason. The problem with rationality, as Iliopoulos explains, derives from the fact that this particular permutation of reason

## Chapter 6. The Reason of Unreason

acknowledges no limit to its powers, thus asserting the absoluteness of its tyranny.

> Kant shows that it is precisely the illegitimate status of sovereignty accorded to rationality which increases our dependence on the authority of another and reinforces our state of tutelage. The attitude of the Enlightenment begins when, by rigorously demarcating the limits of the understanding, reason ensures its legitimate application, rendering the subject autonomous precisely by abolishing the need to appeal to an external authority [Iliopoulos, 2017, pp. 8–9].

By so doing, Kant argues, rationality inherently, paradoxically, violates the terms of its own claim to reason. For is it not the unshakeable rule of reason that reasonable judgments cannot be arbitrary, that they must always follow the rules of logic? Rationality breaks this principle when it arbitrarily declares itself to be reasonable, a contradiction that Foucault will restate in his analysis of the Cogito in the *History of Madness*.

In its detachment from empirical reality, the concept of reason that Kant puts forward in the *Anthropology* provides the same functional space that Felman claims for literature in *Writing and Madness*, a zone into which reason can strategically retreat from the tyranny of the rational so that, by exploring the limits of this escape into unreason, it can reorient itself *as* reason. Reason deploys this tactic to sound the alarm whenever arbitrariness, including its own, threatens to corrupt the rational process. "When this transgression occurs, the rational employment of the faculties disintegrates, leading to phenomena of irrationality, madness," explains Iliopoulos. "It is the task of the anthropology, in contrast to all psychological enterprises, to reflect on the instances when the harmony of the rational functions of consciousness falls apart and the abyss of unreason threatens the consistency of the mind" (Iliopoulos, 2017, p. 11). Through this gesture, the hidden reason of unreason makes its purpose manifest. A strategic withdrawal into the zone of unreason is not a rejection of reason *as such*, but rather a way of renouncing a rationality that has violated its own terms. In these circumstances, it becomes entirely reasonable to be unreasonable.

The concept of madness under consideration, therefore, is not usually undertaken involuntarily, at least not at first. This kind of madness is literary, artistic—it is the madness of Hamlet, of Don Quixote, of Catherine Morland, characters who *perform* madness and, in so doing, step out of the circle of their own rationality in order to see logic from a fresh perspective. Foucault thus argues that madness, when understood as logic's double, opens up the possibility of seeing reason in a new way:

> The madman leaves the path of reason, but by means of the images, beliefs, and forms of reasoning that are equally to be found in men of reason. The madman therefore is never mad to his own way of thinking, but only in the eyes of a third person who can distinguish between reason and the exercise of reason [Foucault, 2006, p. 184].

To enter into the realm of madness, these literary examples show, is to choose unreason for the sake of (and in the name of) reason. "The madness of madness is to be secretly reason," explains Foucault. "And that non-madness, as the content of madness, is the second essential point that must be made about unreason. Unreason is that the truth of madness is reason" (Foucault, 2006, p. 206). The power of unreason is not limited to releasing the subject from the arbitrary cage of human rationality. The artistic dimensions of unreason allow a blurring of the line between first and third person: to perform madness is to enter the zone of the irrational, but it is also to step outside one's self, to imagine who we are, as Foucault puts it, through the "eyes of a third person who can distinguish between reason and the exercise of reason" (Foucault, 2006, p. 184). This third person may be either real (Henry Tilney's role in *Northanger Abbey*, for instance) or imaginary (Don Quixote's eventual realization of his own insanity), but the process of subjective identification and alienation is functionally the same in both cases.

The decision to pass voluntarily into the realm of unreason in Clarke's fiction mirrors the magician's entry into the irrational domain of magic. The parallel between these two actions is reiterated, for instance, in Roxanne Barbara Doerr's chapter "Summons, Prophecies, Possession and Madness: Intersections of Law and Magic in *Jonathan Strange and Mr. Norrell*" (2016), in which the crucial connection between magic and madness is reiterated. "[I]n the realm of magic," explains Doerr, "insanity was appreciated by magicians in the past and seen not as impaired reasoning but rather the means to access otherwise unattainable knowledge" (Doerr, 2016, p. 413). Doerr observes how the interplay between rationality and magic involves an increasingly unstable relationship between the two realms, eventually culminating in Strange's fateful decision to go mad in order to explore the limits of

## Chapter 6. The Reason of Unreason

his magical powers. "[W]hen Strange uses magic to purposely go mad he goes beyond laws and rationality and therefore manages to meet the gentleman with whom he entertains a completely different sort of relation compared to Norrell" (Doerr, 2016, p. 414). Doerr thus contrasts the power and effectiveness of the mad Strange's negotiations to the relative failure of the rational Norrell's attempts to deploy the magic of the fairies.

The sequence in which Strange transforms the extent of his powers by willingly giving himself up to madness is truly, as Doerr suggests, one of the most important sequences in the novel. Explaining its significance is made more difficult by the fact that Clarke is quite vague when it comes to describing how exactly the magicians in her book perform their magic. Norrell, for instance, seems to formulate his spells with the scholarly assistance of his vast library, especially the eminent Francis Sutton-Grove's *De Generibus Artium*, studying iterations of earlier spells with the aim of either repetition or emulation. Strange's method, by contrast, is barely deserving of that name, as his magic springs from an obscure source of inspiration that follows no obvious rules or technique. At his second meeting with Norrell, for instance, when Strange is called upon to demonstrate his talent, he does so by placing a copy of Jeremy Tott's *English Magic* on the other side of the mirror. Like Carroll's Alice, the book travels into the realm of unreason on the other side of the mirror. Despite this impressive practical display, Strange confesses himself profoundly ignorant of the actual process by which he achieved this task (Clarke, 2015, p. 295). Strange's perplexed account of his magical abilities resembles the kind of romantic inspiration found in Coleridge's "The Eolian Harp" (1795), in which technology combines with nature to produce an improvised form of natural music, or Mozart's prodigious ability to create complex spontaneous compositions in his head.

For much of *Jonathan Strange and Mr. Norrell*, the magic that Strange performs is conducted in this instinctive manner. Even his feats at the Battle of Waterloo are carried out via a series of mental associations that Strange then summons by contemplating his surroundings. A crucial turning point in his approach to magic occurs in Chapter 49, at a dinner with Lord Portishead and Sir Walter Pole. After Strange reflects abstrusely about how the madness of the king seems to enhance the latter's communications with the world of the fairies, Sir Walter asks

## English Magic and Imperial Madness

whether such a connection could be cultivated proactively. This simple question plants the seeds of a new approach in Strange's head. As, with increasing excitement, he considers the ramifications of what Sir Walter has said, Strange recalls the magicians of the past and their links to madness. The Aureates, he remembers, used madness as a way of achieving a higher level of magic, with Ralph Stokesey, for instance, matching the wildness of his fairy-servant Col Tom Blue:

> Perhaps I am too tame, too *domestic* a magician. But how *does* one work up a little madness? I meet with mad people every day in the street, but I never thought before to wonder how they got mad. Perhaps I should go wandering on lonely moors and barren shores. That is always a popular place for lunatics—in novels and plays at any rate. Perhaps wild England will make me mad [Clarke, 2015, p. 707].

Although Strange falls back initially on the trope of "wild England," on the ideas familiar from the romantic art and literature of his time, the experience of madness he is looking for turns out to lie not in the splendors of the English countryside, but on the other side of a mirror.

While the most striking place that Strange visits by passing through the mirror is the land of Faerie, there is another destination that Clarke indicates as also belonging to the other side of the mirror: Venice. The magical significance of this city is hinted at early in the novel when Clarke describes the extensive collection of paintings of Venice belonging to Mrs. Wintertowne, which she gives to Walter Pole in anticipation of his marriage to her daughter. These paintings are described as more than simple representations of the city, for they reflect some deeper, more mysterious quality. Clarke describes how, in the gloom of the London winter, these paintings appear less like depictions of Venice than black mirrors that reflect one another (Clarke, 2015, p. 84). As well as these paintings, there are a number of actual Venetian mirrors mentioned in the course of the novel: in Chapter 15, Stephen instructs the servants to hang two Venetian mirrors opposite one another to create an infinite *mise en abyme*, for instance, while the Elizabethan court magician Gregory Absalom decorated his Shadow House "with Turkey carpets and Venetian mirrors and glass and a hundred other beautiful things" (Clarke, 2015, p. 267). The most important reference to a Venetian mirror, however, occurs at the end of Chapter 35, when Strange is asked by a country gentleman what astonishing magical feat he will

## Chapter 6. The Reason of Unreason

perform next. Walter Pole replies in his place by nodding "in the direction of a large Venetian mirror which took up most of one wall and was at that moment reflecting only darkness, and he declared, 'He will walk into that mirror and he will not come out again'" (Clarke, 2015, p. 493). Strange, in effect, replicates the magical feat he had earlier demonstrated to Norrell, except that instead of a book titled *English Magic* passing through the looking glass, it will now be himself.

This narrative thread culminates when Strange, having departed England for the European continent, takes up residence in Venice in the company of the Greysteel family. Upon their arrival in Venice, the Greysteels, having received a letter from a mutual friend asking them to check in on an elderly relative, travel to the Ghetto to visit a Mrs. Delgado. Strange accompanies them on this errand and quickly realizes that Mrs. Delgado, who lives in an attic compartment with dozens of cats, is completely insane. In a subsequent conversation with Miss Greysteel, in which she asks if it would be possible for Strange to cure Mrs. Delgado using magic, he reaffirms Norrell's earlier observation that magic is too close to madness to serve as an effective remedy. Mrs. Delgado's condition nonetheless provides Strange with the opportunity suggested by Sir Walter, and so he later returns alone to her apartment with the aim of fulfilling his intention of going mad:

> "I want you to teach me how to be mad. The idea is so simple, I wonder I did not think of it before." Mrs. Delgado growled very low. "Oh! You question the wisdom of my proceedings? You are probably right. To wish madness upon oneself is very rash" [Clarke, 2015, p. 763].

Strange requests from the old woman "something to serve as a symbol and vessel of your madness" (Clarke, 2015, p. 763) and discovers it in the form of a dead mouse lying on a saucer nearby. He then casts his spell and transforms Mrs. Delgado, first into several earlier incarnations from her life and then, finally, into a small, gray cat. This physical metamorphosis completes the feline transformation the old woman had already achieved in her mind.

Examining this episode carefully reveals the underlying logic of Strange's spells. The key to their success derives from an initial linguistic association, which is then metamorphosed by magic into reality—recall, for instance, Strange's spectacular rescue of the sailors stranded on the *False Prelate*, an English ship that has run aground and is in danger of

## English Magic and Imperial Madness

breaking up. The solution to that problem comes to Strange when he learns the name of the shoal on which the ship is stranded: Horse Sand. Strange turns this name from a metaphor into a real object, transforming the sand into animated horses that use their strength to dislodge the ship. This same logic is at work, albeit more subtly, in the case of Mrs. Delgado, whose name is a derivation of the Italian phrase *"del gatto,"* which means "of the cat." Clarke accentuates the importance of language to the old lady's metamorphosis by relating, in a footnote at the end of Chapter 52, how Mrs. Delgado had been a master of many tongues, until "a great wind of madness howled through her and overturned all her languages" and she "forgot every thing in the world except Cat—and that it is said, she spoke marvellously well" (Clarke, 2015, p. 754). A slippage between language and reality occurs repeatedly in Strange's magic, so that his spells are a kind of pun, a concretized play on words that recalls *Through the Looking Glass*—think of Carroll's humorous inventions of the "bread-and-butter-fly" and the "rocking-horse-fly" in Chapter 3 of that work, for instance (Carroll, 1998, pp. 85–86). In Strange's magic, therefore, language is temporarily released from the boundaries of the symbolic by a slippage of meaning (a pun, a mental association) that somehow, magically, allows it to invade reality.

The actions that Strange undertakes immediately after Mrs. Delgado's transformation into a cat are the culmination of Clarke's exploration of the connection between magic and madness. Lifting up the dead mouse from the saucer, Strange decides that, in order to take advantage of the path of madness revealed to him by his visit to Mrs. Delgado, he must ingest this symbolic offering—not for himself, but for the sake of English magic (Clarke, 2015, p. 764). This gesture works for Strange, greatly expanding his magical powers at the expense of his reason. The grotesque act of eating a dead mouse is not an arbitrary fictional device invented by Clarke, but is chosen from historical precedent—in the medieval period, eating a dead mouse was recommended as a prevalent *cure* for madness. One of the most widely cited examples of this remedy comes from Pope John XXI (1215–1277), who advocates it in his *Thesaurus Pauperum* (*Treasures of the Poor*), a handbook for common diseases.

Yet it is the rise of madness as the supposedly "English malady" in the Elizabethan period that provides the strongest connection to Clarke's parallel exploration of "English magic." The significance of Strange's ingestion of the mouse in search of the madness that underlies

## Chapter 6. The Reason of Unreason

English magic ought to be understood in the light of this historical link. Strange does not eat the mouse whole—he grinds it up and mixes it with brandy to produce a tincture of madness, the strength of which can be measured in drops. In the wake of this experiment, Strange writes a series of fevered letters to his brother-in-law, Henry Woodhope, in which he exclaims: "Madness is the key. I believe I am the first English magician to understand that. Norrell was right—he said we do not need fairies to help us" (Clarke, 2015, p. 828). To choose madness deliberately, to step beyond the bounds of reason is Strange's most revolutionary moment, his Reformation of English magic, in which it becomes appropriate to unleash the full power of magic without the mediation of fairies.

The allusion to Henry Woodhope provides one final clue to this narrative arc, pointing the reader beyond the text of *Jonathan Strange and Mr. Norrell* to Clarke's story "The Ladies of Grace Adieu." Although "The Ladies of Grace Adieu" was published in 2006, this piece was actually the first published text to take place in the fictional universe of Strange and Norrell. Set during a visit by Strange and Arabella to the latter's brother, Clarke's tale focuses on a trio of female magicians: Cassandra Parbringer, Miss Tobias, and Mrs. Fields. The way in which these three women practice magic is strikingly different from their male counterparts. "Clarke's women assert themselves as legitimate channels for magic, denying its more conservative, masculine strain and offering an organic view of England's magical heritage," contends Victoria Hoyle, "they are more 'in touch' with the forces of otherness that encircle human lives than either Strange or Norell. They're on the margins, but they're 'naturals' and they're pro-active" (Hoyle, 2006). In the course of the story, the reader discovers that the women have the magical ability to transform themselves into owls and their enemies into mice, in what turns out to be a foreshadowing of the encounter between Strange and Mrs. Delgado:

> "We have found some bones," said his wife, with a puzzled air. "Small, white bones, it would seem, of some delicate little creatures, and two little grey skins like empty pods. Come, sir, you are the magician, explain it to us."
>
> "They are mouse bones. And mouse skins too. It is owls that do that. See," said Strange, "the skins are turned quite inside out. Curious, is it not?"

## English Magic and Imperial Madness

> Mrs Strange was not greatly impressed with this as an explanation. "So I dare say," she said, "but what seems to me far more miraculous is that we found these bones in the cloaths which Miss Parbringer and Mrs Field had to wipe their fingers and their mouths. Jonathan, I hope you are not suggesting that these ladies have been eating mice?" [Clarke, 2007b, p. 31].

The depth of Clarke's subversion can be felt, as Hoyle puts it, in the "precise, clean, and cold" aspects of "Clarke's portrayal of 'women's magic' in this story," which is "urgent and desperate, but it is also natural and in the course of things" (Hoyle, 2006). The cool rationality of the trio of female magicians who regularly devour mice in "The Ladies of Grace Adieu" bears little resemblance to the melodrama of Strange's emotional meltdown after just a few drops from the tincture.

Nonetheless, it is the decision of Jonathan Strange to go mad deliberately, to plunge himself into the realm of unreason, that crucially pulls together the intertwining notions of the "English malady" and its connection in the novel to the power of "English magic." Norrell is the one who, in his early conversations with Strange on this topic, provides the theoretical basis for a link between magic and madness, but it is Strange who proves its truth through the experiment he performs on himself. Strange thus unveils unreason as reason's double, undertaking a necessary journey to the other side of the looking-glass, not for the sake of insanity itself, but to deploy its power as a restorative tool.

# Epilogue: New Constellations

## *The Starry Heavens*

At the grave of Immanuel Kant in Kaliningrad, there is a commemorative plaque in German and Russian that reads: "Two things fill the mind with ever new and increasing admiration and reverence, the more often and more steadily one reflects on them: *the starry heavens above me and the moral law within me*" (Kant, 1997, p. 133). These famous lines are taken from Kant's *Critique of Practical Reason* (1788), and they are an affirmation of the divine order of things. Just as God has fixed the stars in their eternal places, so too he has inscribed his ethical laws, grounded in reason, onto the hearts and minds of the human race. Despite its appeal to seemingly timeless categories (stars, reason), Kant's moral philosophy in truth abolishes centuries of thinking about the law and its relation to the good. The categorical imperative in *Critique of Practical Reason* disconnects the ethical aim from its outcome, so that what matters is not whether a moral action is good, but whether the logical form of the law has been followed, as Gilles Deleuze explains in *Coldness and Cruelty* (1966):

> In the *Critique of Practical Reason* Kant gave a rigorous formulation of a radically new conception, in which the law is no longer regarded as dependent on the Good, but on the contrary, the Good itself is made to depend on the law. This means that the law no longer has its foundation in some higher principle from which it would derive its authority, but that it is self-grounded and valid solely by virtue of its own form. For the first time we can now speak of THE LAW, regarded as an absolute, without further specification or reference to an object. Whereas the classical conception only dealt with *the laws* according to the various spheres of the Good or the various circumstances attending the Best, Kant can speak of the moral law, and of its application to what otherwise remains

## Epilogue: New Constellations

totally undetermined. The moral law is the representation of a pure form and is independent of content or object, spheres of activity or circumstances [Deleuze, 1989, pp. 82–83].

This Kantian conception of the law, grounded in the rational rather than the good, means that the "object of the law is by definition unknowable and elusive" (Deleuze, 1989, p. 83): the law instructs us *how* to behave according to abstract principles, but it does not tell us why, or to what end. As such, Deleuze points out, the law "defines a realm of transgression where one is already guilty, and where one oversteps the bounds without knowing what they are" (Deleuze, 1989, pp. 83–84). The paradoxes of this situation have been extensively explored in literature: Deleuze points to Franz Kafka's *The Trial* (1925), in which a bemused Josef K. experiences a profound sense of guilt despite having no idea what his crime might be, and the Marquis de Sade's *Justine* (1791), whose eponymous heroine blindly follows every virtuous principle yet is repeatedly "punished" for her goodness, ending in her random death by a bolt of lightning. This pattern of protagonists acting without full knowledge of the significance of their actions is repeated in *Jonathan Strange and Mr. Norrell*, culminating with Clarke's revelation that the return of English magic has, from the outset, been the work of the Raven King, and that Strange and Norrell were only ever his puppets.

Clarke nonetheless strongly implies that the return of the Raven King will not be a straightforward restoration, that things cannot simply, miraculously return to how they were during John Uskglass's earlier reign. The Raven King, after all, is bringing with him, in the form of English magic, an unreasonable antidote to the tyranny of rationality. Kant's memorable line about *"the starry heavens above me and the moral law within me"* (Kant, 1997, p. 133) thus proves to be unsustainable as both a metaphor and a system of ethical thought. What Kant naively prizes about the stars is their unchanging fixity, their value as a metaphor of the invariable nature of rationality, without realizing that stars (as well as the earth from which we observe those stars) are actually in a constant state of motion. Clarke signals the enormity of the events that are unfolding in her novel by having the stars move out of their constellations. "The stars were shifting and changing;" she writes in the novel's concluding pages, "in the patch of sky above them were new constellations" (Clarke, 2015, p. 1004). This device disrupts not only the key symbol of modern Kantian ethics, but also the tradition of English

## Epilogue: New Constellations

prophecy. Astrology, predicated on the ability to read the stars, emerged as one of the foremost intellectual discourses of the medieval period, with Thomas observing in *Religion and the Decline of Magic* that it was

> less a separate discipline than an aspect of a generally accepted world picture. It was necessary for the understanding of physiology and therefore of medicine. It taught of the influence of the stars upon the plants and minerals, and therefore shaped botany and metallurgy. Psychology and ethnography also presupposed a good deal of astrological dogma. During the Renaissance, even more than in the Middle Ages, astrology pervaded all aspects of scientific thought. It was not a coterie doctrine, but an essential aspect of the intellectual framework in which men were educated. Nevertheless, the subject had a life and independent momentum of its own, especially when the prestige of the Ptolemaic picture of the universe began to crumble under the pressure of the astronomical discoveries of the century and a half between Copernicus and Newton [Thomas, 2003, p. 338].

Whereas the narrative of disenchantment regards astrology and science as inherently opposed, authors like Thomas have shown that, historically, this was not the case, that magical disciplines like astrology were the intellectual foundations from which modern science grew and developed. A disruption in the stars, therefore, represents a major symbolic shift, a sidereal revolution to rival that of Copernicus.

Consider, for instance, the central role that Merlin plays in the English prophetic tradition. Merlin was a natural magician, but one of his most important powers was his ability to divine the future. Indeed, the most famous section of Geoffrey of Monmouth's *The History of the Kings of Britain* is an interlude, written in obscure and poetic language, that purported to be a series of prophecies by Merlin about the future of England. At the time of the country's greatest crisis, Merlin proclaims, the stars will shift from their constellations. "Men will become drunk with the wine which is offered to them: they will turn their backs on Heaven and fix their eyes on the earth," writes Geoffrey. "The stars will avert their gaze from these men and alter their accustomed course" (Monmouth, 1977, p. 184). What Merlin is predicting here is a kind of apocalypse, an end to the celestial order, in which the stars become untethered from their divinely ordained places, a symptom of the world ending and the implied imminence of the Second Coming of Christ—a

## Epilogue: New Constellations

theme that Clarke appropriates and transforms into the return of the Raven King and English magic.

Long before the dramatic formation of these new constellations in the latter parts of *Jonathan Strange and Mr. Norrell*, however, various clues foreshadow the disintegration of the old sidereal order. When Arabella goes missing, for instance, Strange uses a technique known as scrying, which involves gazing on a reflective surface, such as a mirror or a bowl of water, to divine the location of his wife. On this occasion, Clarke pointedly connects the scrying process to the arrangement of the stars:

> He drew his finger over the surface of the water twice. Two glittering lines of light appeared, quartering the water. He made a gesture above one of the quarters. Stars appeared in it and more lines, veinings and webs of light. He stared at this for some moments. Then he made a gesture above the next quarter. A different pattern of light appeared. He repeated the process for the third and fourth quarters. The patterns did not remain the same. They shifted and sparkled, sometimes appearing like writing, at other times like the lines of a map and at other times like constellations of stars [Clarke, 2015, p. 625].

Whereas this technique in the novel had previously proven to be a reliable tool for surveillance—Strange uses it on several occasions as a weapon against the French, for instance—the intervention of the gentleman with the thistledown hair, and the impending return of English magic, mark the beginning of a prophesied disruption that is prefigured in Strange's personal life by the abduction of Arabella.

The unusual movements of the stars thus become increasingly noteworthy as the novel moves toward its conclusion, such as when Drawlight, having been sent on a mission to Venice, attempts to use his unctuous tactics on Dr. Greysteel's manservant, Frank. To trick Drawlight into revealing his nefarious plans, Frank initially pretends to be interested in the cowardly villain's words, then proceeds to kick Drawlight into the canal. Pulled along by a magical current, Drawlight eventually washes up near the dark tower inhabited by Strange, who has been driven out of his wits by his quest to discover a magic powerful enough to retrieve Arabella. When Drawlight gazes up at the night sky, he makes a startling discovery:

> The only live, bright things were the stars. Their constellations looked to Drawlight like gigantic, glittering letters—letters in an unknown

alphabet. For all he knew the magician had formed the stars into these letters and used them to write a spell against him. All that could be seen in any direction was black Night, stars and silence [Clarke, 2015, p. 852].

These signs are portents, not only of the return of the Raven King, but of something larger, more thematic going on in Clarke's novel. As a symbol, the movement of the stars out of their constellations represents a new dawn in human history, announced by the signifier of Endless Night that surrounds Strange's tower.

## *Endless Night*

We have already seen that Merlin, in *The History of the Kings of Britain*, prophesies that the "stars will avert their gaze from these men and alter their accustomed course" (Monmouth, 1977, p. 184). This line also needs to be read, however, in the context of what happens to Merlin in Geoffrey of Monmouth's later work *The Life of Merlin*, which not only gives a clearer picture of his prophetic abilities and how they are connected to his astrological knowledge, but also anticipates Strange's narrative trajectory. Like Strange, Merlin's magical ability to read the stars in order to predict the future is greatly enhanced by a bout of insanity:

> [O]bservation of the stars, and interpretation of the results, are associated with the theme of Merlin's madness. It is when Merlin is alienated from other humans and refusing to have contact with kings and their courts that astrology plays the strongest part in his story. The first example comes when Merlin is so deeply insane that he is described as living like an animal. Even so, he is capable of watching "the stars in their courses" and interpreting their movements [Lawrence-Mathers, 2012, p. 98].

While still living like a madman in the forest, Merlin asks his sister, Queen Ganieda, to build him an astrological observatory from which he can study the stars and predict the fate of England.

> So raise me a house, send me retainers to serve me and prepare meals in the time when the earth refuses its grain and the tree its fruit. Before the other buildings build me a remote one to which you will seventy doors and as many windows, through which I may see firebreathing Phoebus with Venus, and watch by night the stars wheeling in the firmament; and they will teach me about the future of the nation [Monmouth, 1973, p. 83].

## Epilogue: New Constellations

Merlin's observatory is the literary precursor of Strange's magical tower, the latter surrounded by a thick layer of darkness that Clarke describes as "Endless Night" (Clarke, 2015, p. 816). In Chapter 8 of *The Life of Merlin*, Merlin is visited by the legendary Welsh poet Taliesin who, with the help of Minerva, delivers a long exposition about the nature of heaven and earth, in the course of which he mentions how at "the latitude of ultima Thule, this is also the time at which there is 'endless night'" (Lawrence-Mathers, 2012, p. 101).

This reference to "endless night" shows up again centuries later in English literature, in one of the most famous lines of the poet William Blake, who writes in "Auguries of Innocence" (1803): "Some are Born to sweet delight/Some are Born to Endless Night" (Blake, 2004, p. 510). Blake may be regarded here as a contemporary counterpoint to Kant, the moral conservatism of the "starry night" standing in contrast to the revolution of "eternal night." Indeed, in his study *William Blake* (1933), John Middleton Murry interprets Blake's *The French Revolution* (1791) through this very opposition. "It is the Law, in Blake's most comprehensive meaning, that is being challenged and overthrown by the French Revolution," writes Murry. "By the Law the starry hosts have been fixed in their places, the Infinite made finite, until the heavens are as a palace built of marble" (Murry, 1971, p. 55). The words spoken in Blake's poem by the Duke of Burgundy are "also unconsciously echoing the cold ecstasy of Kant when he identified the Law of the starry heavens above us with the Moral Law within," he continues. "The 'categorical imperative,' whether enthroned in the visible authority of the Catholic Church, or the invisible authority of the Practical Reason, is what Revolution, in Blake's meaning, must overthrow" (Murry, 1971, p. 56). Blake's words are thus inscribed in a prophetic and apocalyptic vision, in which the stars, as the symbol of the old order, come unmoored from their settings.

The significance of Blake's words becomes clearer in the larger context of his poems, which continue to explore the consequences of spiritual revolution for the world as a whole. Blake lays the foundations of this vision in three subsequent works—*America: A Prophecy* (1793), *Europe: A Prophecy* (1794), and *The Song of Los* (1795), with this last text divided into two sections, "Africa" and "Asia." The true culmination of this idea arrives in the later poem *Jerusalem: The Emanation of the Great Albion*, which Blake began in 1804 and continued to work on until 1820.

## Epilogue: New Constellations

Drawing on the English tradition of intertwining history and mythology, in *Jerusalem* Blake draws together a heterogeneous mixture of stories, overcoding earlier pagan elements, such as the Druids, with a Christian apocalyptic narrative in which England—referred to here by its ancient name of Albion—becomes the true holy land, with the English as God's chosen people:

> Jerusalem the Emanation of the Giant Albion! Can it be? Is it a Truth that the Learned have explored? Was Britain the Primitive Seat of the Patriarchal Religion? If it is true: my title-page is also True, that Jerusalem was & is the Emanation of the Giant Albion. It is True, and cannot be controverted. Ye are united O ye inhabitants of Earth in One Religion.
> [...]
> "All things Begin & End in Albions Ancient Druid Rocky Shore."
> Your Ancestors derived their origin from Abraham, Heber, Shem, and Noah, who were Druids: as the Druid Temples (which are the Patriarchal Pillars & Oak Groves) over the whole Earth witness to this day [Blake, 2004, p. 685].

In Blake's poem, therefore, it is the old certainties that are coming apart, so that "now the Starry Heavens are fled from the mighty limbs of Albion" (Blake, 2004, p. 686). Heavily influenced by John Milton's unfinished *The History of Britain* (1670), Blake prophesies in *Jerusalem* a final transition to the "One Religion. The Religion of Jesus: the most Ancient, the Eternal: & the Everlasting Gospel" (Blake, 2004, p. 685), with Albion/England at its center.

Unlike many of his contemporaries, the political status that Blake enjoys today is mainly positive, a reputation that is due, in large part, to his abolitionist stance against slavery, evident in the compassion he expresses in "The Little Black Boy," one of the most famous poems from *Songs of Innocence* (1789), and his antinomian views on everything from religion to sexuality to clothing (Blake was an early advocate of nudism). Yet because the notion of "Englishness" is so wrapped up in England's imperial connotations, there are always moral ambiguities and pitfalls in writing about its national mythologies. Blake's work, for all its dazzling ability to question political and religious dogma, is ultimately unable to escape entirely from this problem, so that even among its affirmations of radical emancipation there are racist and colonial tropes woven into the fabric of his texts. The Albion that he imagines emerging in *Jerusalem* may be a spiritual empire, but it is still an empire, one that bears

## Epilogue: New Constellations

an uncomfortable resemblance to the actual imperial project of the English.

Blake nonetheless remains a fascinating figure because, like Clarke, instead of succumbing passively to ideology, his work engages in a powerful struggle with its own mythology. What is particularly striking about this resistance is the central role played by Blake's critique of reason. The aftermath of the fall of Albion (England), for instance, which is examined in *The Four Zoas* (1797–1807), features an emblematic character named Urizen; Urizen is also the focus of an earlier text by Blake, *The Book of Urizen* (1794). The symbolism of Urizen's name can be detected by saying it aloud—"your reason"—and this figure represents, for Blake, the fallen state of humanity. Humanity's misery proceeds from its sin of intellectual pride, a rational solipsism that prevents it from enjoying the consolations of natural religion. The character of Urizen represents a human reason that, by turning on itself, has been corrupted into unreason. Paul Youngquist writes in "Vision, Madness, Myth and William Blake" (1994):

> The act of creation in *The Book of Urizen* represents not so much the *fall* of God as his *birth*, which Blake presents as a species of madness, the dissociation of a unified psyche. In the original division that separates Urizen from eternity, a mentality is born whose individual avatar is self-consciousness and whose collective representation is the jealous god of antiquity. The unsettling implication of this theogony is that such a god comes into being through a pathological division in the mind. Blake traces this division to its logical conclusion in madness [Youngquist, 1994, p. 123].

Urizen thus performs a similar function in Blake's mythology to Satan in Milton's *Paradise Lost* (1667), his fallen state providing a fascinating retreat from the tyranny of reason in a move that allows the poet to explore the twilight world—or perhaps more pertinently, the Eternal Night—of unreason.

## *Beyond Disenchantment*

The apparent opposition between the light of the stars and endless night, between rationality and madness, even between the ethical systems of Kant and Blake, forms a crucial motif in *Jonathan Strange*

## Epilogue: New Constellations

*and Mr. Norrell*. Despite the attempts of reason to isolate itself, to establish its autonomous purity, unreason nonetheless haunts reason like a shadow. Foucault was wrong to believe that madness had been reduced to silence, for the historical truth is that unreason, even when outwardly suppressed, has never ceased to speak. Indeed, the radical attempt by reason to isolate itself, to address a mad soliloquy to itself about how rational it is, ought to be understood as an explosion of unreason. Do we not hear an echo of Blake's Urizen in this absurd attempt at logical purity, in which reason solipsistically turns on itself? Or closer to home, is it not just like the bizarrely meandering narratives spoken by Lady Pole or Stephen? The mad are not reduced to silence in Clarke's novel, after all. Instead, their stories are drained of all significance to both speaker and listener, so that their outward coherence (reason) is juxtaposed to their status as nonsense (unreason). These examples are the outcome of a long history of the repeated, foolhardy attempt to detach reason from unreason in a vain attempt to make it "pure."

One of the key innovations of the myth of disenchantment was to map this dichotomy of reason and unreason onto a defining antagonism that associated science with the rational and magic (or religion) with the irrational. The putative obviousness of this conceptual separation, its acceptance as conventional wisdom, can only be truly unsettled by a knowledge of history. For if the disenchantment narrative is correct, then science ought to have developed outside of, and in opposition to, the discourses of religion and magic. Yet even a passing knowledge of the history of science shows that this is simply not true, that magic and religion were crucial in setting the parameters of scientific thought. For Francis Bacon, for example, the modern division between science and magic would have been meaningless, since the concept of magic referred to "natural magic," the ability to manipulate the physical world, an approach that foregrounded both experimentation and technology. In his book *Knowledge is Power* (2017), John Henry thus observes:

> The simple truth is that modern historians have not properly understood the magical tradition. In particular they have failed to grasp what was meant by the term "natural magic." There was nothing irrational in Bacon's day in believing in magic. The belief that bodies had specific properties and virtues that enabled them to act upon or interact with other bodies to bring about particular ends entirely conforms with modern beliefs. [...] [T]o deny what then seemed to be the natural hierarchies

## Epilogue: New Constellations

in things [...] was to descend beyond the merely irrational to sheer madness. Nor was it irrational to believe that by intoning a special combination of words, a magic spell or incantation, remarkable physical effects could be produced [Henry, 2017, p. 80].

Mordechai Feingold, in his article "'And Knowledge Shall Be Increased': Millenarianism and the Advancement of Learning Revisited" (2013), further examines the religious ideas that so heavily shaped Bacon's thinking, from the impending sense in the seventeenth century that the Apocalypse was rapidly approaching, to Bacon's desire to create a science that would recapture the perfection of human knowledge as it existed before the Fall. Greenwood thus points out that the disenchantment narrative, when examined through a historically-informed perspective of what actually took place, is factually wrong, for "magic did not give way to religion and science; rather, the practical and experimental aspects of magic were adopted by science, and many of the ideas inherent in sympathetic magic were absorbed" (Greenwood, 2009, p. 50). The antagonistic opposition between magic and science is an invention after the fact, a reflection of modern prejudices rather than a historically accurate picture of how these two discourses actually developed.

Clarke's masterstroke is to undermine the myth of disenchantment, not by showing that enchantment still exists in the world, but by subversively mapping the logic of disenchantment onto the return of English magic. The modern magic that Norrell wishes to promote is a form of magic that claims to "return" to an earlier state while at the same time, with Norrell's exclusion of the Raven King and fairy magic, performing the revolutionary act of rewriting the past in such a way that a true return becomes impossible. Norrell wants to create a modern English magic that is bourgeois and rational, that purges the term of its connection to anything that is not dry and scholarly. Strange is the romantic riposte to this disenchanted form of magic, the fictional source of inspiration for Byron's verse drama *Manfred* (1817). The split between Clarke's two magicians creates an artificial division between their followers, a divergence so prominent that, as the novel moves toward its conclusion, Clarke shows how the world has also come to accept this breach as a "natural" division. Childermass, for instance, gathers a group of magicians together to show them the magical book inscribed on Vinculus's body, and the members of his audience are, without exception, adherents of one of these two schools, divided into Strangites and Norrellites despite their never having even met either of those two magicians (Clarke, 2015, p. 1000). This "natural" antagonism between the two magicians overlooks the fact that, well beyond the halfway mark of the novel, Strange and Norrell formed a kind of "partnership" (Clarke, 2015, p. 534) based on their mutual interest in magic. The return of English magic helmed by Norrell only *later* faces a challenge from Strange and his disciples who, in championing the Raven King as the true emblem of English magic, see themselves as enacting a more authentic form of return. The conclusion of the novel finally overthrows the dichotomy between the two magicians, as revealed in a crucial conversation between Childermass and Vinculus at the end of Chapter 67:

> "Norrell is a clever man—and Strange another. They have their faults, as other men do, but their achievements are still remarkable. Make no mistake; I am John Uskglass's man. Or would be, if he were here. But you must admit that the restoration of English magic is their work, not his."
> "Their work!" scoffed Vinculus. "Theirs? Do you still not understand? They *are* the spell John Uskglass is doing. That is all they have ever been. And he is doing it now!" [Clarke, 2015, p. 975].

With this disclosure, Vinculus causes the antagonism between Strange and Norrell to dissolve. It turns out that our two protagonists, for all their bickering and disagreements, have never *not* been doing the magic of the Raven King. In much the same way, humans living in the modern world have never been disenchanted, nor have we have ever been truly rational. The modern secular enterprise was built on a false premise, a fabricated narrative of reason's emergence that, just as Byron does in his reimagining of Strange as Manfred, fits itself to the heroic image of cool rationality that we wanted to believe of ourselves, an imaginary phantom sustained by the mythology of disenchantment.

## *The Sky Speaks*

Just because we see through the false premises of the myth of disenchantment does not mean that we can now see clearly and distinctly. We must never deceive ourselves into thinking that we have entered into a clear and comprehensive understanding: there is no "pure" reason, since reason and unreason are inextricably tied together. Any form of

## Epilogue: New Constellations

rationality that attempts to achieve purity by isolating itself in this way ends up contradicting itself, to the point where it can only drive itself mad *in the name of reason*. Felman argues in *Writing and Madness* that literature is a crucial antidote to this tendency of reason to turn against itself, because fiction provides a space where reason and unreason can coexist. One of the great errors of modern criticism, she points out, has been the attempt to truncate this potential by submitting fiction to a regime of truth and rationality:

> In seeking to "explain" and *master* literature, in refusing, that is, to become a *dupe* of literature, in killing within literature that which makes it literature [...] the psychoanalytic reading, ironically enough, turns out to be a reading that *represses the unconscious*, that represses, paradoxically, the unconscious it purports to be "explaining." To *master*, then (to become the Master), is, here as elsewhere, to *refuse to read* the letters; here as elsewhere, to "see it all" is in effect to "shut one's eyes as tight as possible to the truth"; once more, "to see it all" is in reality to *exclude*; and to exclude, specifically, the unconscious [Felman, 2003, p. 234].

This kind of literary criticism refuses to acknowledge that there are elements of the text that it does not understand, that cannot be explained—that escape, in short, the totalizing aims of its rational hermeneutic. "[T]he psychoanalytical (or critical) *demystification*, paradoxically enough, ends up reproducing the literary *mystification*," continues Felman. "The very thrust of the mystification was, then, to make us believe that there is a radical difference and opposition between the turn of the screw of mystification and the turn of the screw of demystification. But here it is precisely literature's mystification that demystifies and catches the 'demystifier,' by actively, in turn, *mystifying him*" (Felman, 2003, p. 242). This is a similar trap to the one that ensnared earlier critics of the myth of disenchantment, including Adorno and Horkheimer, whose innovative ploy of turning the logic of disenchantment back on itself ultimately failed by naively replicating the logic of mythology. "[N]ot only is myth myth; not only is the opposition to myth myth; *but the recognition of the opposition to myth as myth* is itself myth," observes Josephson-Storm (Josephson-Storm, 2017, p. 10). In short, a critique of the narrative of disenchantment in any of its permutations is bound to fail, because the square on which it eventually lands is always that of myth.

To read *Jonathan Strange and Mr. Norrell* without falling into a

## Epilogue: New Constellations

similar trap, therefore, it is necessary to take seriously Felman's notion of literature as a space that allows us to experience simultaneously the interweaving of reason and unreason. Such an approach does not mean that we can simply jettison the rational, but rather that we must recognize that the rational approach has its limitations, that a reading of the text can never be total. Indeed, Clarke hints at many points that understanding and incomprehension necessarily coexist in the world she has created: the Raven King's prophecy, spoken through the mouthpiece of Vinculus, states that even though magic is written on the branch of every tree, humanity will inevitably fail to comprehend its meaning (Clarke, 2015, pp. 153–154). John Uskglass's prediction is a metatextual guide for how to read Clarke's novel. Such coincidences of simultaneous understanding and puzzlement form a recurrent motif in the novel, a double movement in which Clarke simultaneously reveals *and* conceals what is happening.

Childermass is frequently the target of these coded and unstable revelations. When he visits Vinculus in Chapter 21, for example, the street magician wants to use Childermass's tarot deck to undertake a reading of Norrell's future. Childermass retorts that Vinculus cannot possibly understand the cards he is laying down, but the latter goes ahead with the reading anyway (Clarke, 2015, p. 238). The tarot reading forms another kind of metatext, a story within a story, in which Clarke provides hints of what is to come in the larger narrative. "Though not always orthodox, the reading is highly symbolic of the subsequent adventures of the novel and affects the reader's interpretation of the characters involved," observes Laity. "She lays the ground for the eventual revelation of the Raven King himself, but also of the forthcoming conflicts between the two magicians and their cohorts. Like all good authors, she seeks to lead her readers to make assumptions, but ultimately she holds all the cards herself, so logic often leads to incorrect guesses about the outcomes of the story" (Laity, 2018, p. 220). As Vinculus's reading nears its culmination, the cards magically transform, so that the card marked as *IIII. L'Empereur* turns up multiple times, at which point it then mutates into the recurring figure of the Raven King. The Emperor card represents order and authority, and yet this meaning is belied by the disruptive intrusion of the Raven King. Vinculus's reading thus starts out by following all the usual rules while also surreptitiously flouting them, a mixture of outward convention and inner

## Epilogue: New Constellations

subversion that mirrors the spirit of Clarke's novel. These contradictory glimpses of meaning are shown to the reader, only to be withdrawn and hidden a moment later.

The uncanny effect on Childermass of the tarot deck's metamorphosis recurs more powerfully still in Chapter 46. Clarke begins Volume 3 of the novel, titled "John Uskglass," with several stylistic innovations. The first chapter in this volume, Chapter 45, is an excerpt from Strange's book *The History and Practice of English Magic*, suspending the usual narrative voice to give his words precedence. The succeeding chapter continues this experiment in style, for while a conventional opening paragraph briefly outlines the scene the reader is observing—Childermass sitting in Norrell's library, writing business letters on his master's behalf—the narrative is again suspended, replaced by an excerpt from Childermass's epistle. This text is interrupted, in turn, by a sudden eruption of magic and madness, represented in the novel by the tolling of a bell: what appears next is a brief paragraph written in italics that forcefully inserts itself into Childermass's mind, a thought from outside. For the following two pages, the narrative switches back and forth between Childermass's letters and these mad, intrusive thoughts, reason and unreason existing side by side until, in a moment reminiscent of Descartes's contemplation of the evil demon, he finally breaks out of the reverie and gazes around him. "All the old, familiar objects were there: the shelves of books, the mirror, the ink pot, the fire-irons, the porcelain figure of Martin Pale," writes Clarke. "But his confidence in his own senses was shaken. He no longer trusted that the books, the mirrors, the porcelain figure were really there" (Clarke, 2015, p. 646). These intrusions of unreason into the text drastically change Childermass's perspective on the world around him, for suddenly everything seems to burst with meaning—but a meaning that is beyond the grasp of his understanding:

> *The brown fields were partly flooded; they were strung with chains of chill, grey pools. The pattern of the pools had meaning. The pools had been written on to the fields by the rain. The pools were a magic worked by the rain, just as the tumbling of the black birds against the grey was a spell that the sky was working and the motion of grey-brown grasses was a spell that the wind made. Everything had meaning* [Clarke, 2015, p. 646].

Childermass rings for Norrell's servant, Lucas, and the latter notices Childermass's agitated condition. Just as Childermass is about to

## Epilogue: New Constellations

protest that there is nothing physically wrong with him, another eruption occurs:

> *The sky spoke to him.*
> *It was a language he had never heard before. He was not even certain there were words. Perhaps it only spoke to him in the black writing the birds made. He was small and unprotected and there was no escape. He was caught between earth and sky as if cupped between two hands. They could crush him if they chose.*
> *The sky spoke to him again.*
> *"I do not understand,"* he said [Clarke, 2015, p. 648].

The vertigo that Childermass experiences comes from the way Clarke makes visible the impurity of understanding, with Childermass suspended in a state that is between reason and unreason, instinctively grasping what is happening, yet unable to articulate consciously what is going on. His existence in two realms at once, in Faerie and England, symbolizes this dual zone of reason and unreason that is the true, impure state of human understanding.

Underlying this shift in perspective is Clarke's attempt to articulate an ethical vision. When reason refuses to acknowledge that unreason has a valid purpose and function in the regulation of rationality it becomes tyrannical, insisting on its authority in a way that inherently contradicts its own logic of reasonableness. Throughout *Jonathan Strange and Mr. Norrell,* Clarke uses the return of English magic to examine how this discourse of rationality has been mapped onto national mythologies of Englishness. The English projection of rational virtue and benevolence is used to justify the imperial notion that the English are the natural rulers of their colonized subjects. Thus, the British Empire avowed its own virtues of wisdom and benevolence, even as it indulged in monstrous acts of genocide, slavery, and economic exploitation against peoples the English considered to be inherently inferior. The glaring disparity between the evils of English imperialism and this continuing rhetoric of rational benevolence is itself an act of madness, the true epitome of the "English malady."

That is why, as an English writer herself, Clarke emphasizes the importance of the eccentric movement of the stars as the novel moves toward its conclusion. This change in the night sky, as signaled by Geoffrey of Monmouth's deployment of astrology, is an ancient sign of a

## Epilogue: New Constellations

world coming to an end, and a prophetic indication that a new world of possibility is in the process of being born. The old notion of Englishness, grounded in overblown self-regard and racist imperialism, is hopefully passing away. That is why Childermass, after taking a moral stand against the corrupt figure of Lascelles, is shown glancing at the night sky while making his final departure from Norrell's house:

> Directly above the park and house there was a patch of night-sky shoved in where it did not belong. The constellations were broken. New stars hung there—stars that Childermass had never seen before. They were, presumably, the stars of Strange's Eternal Darkness. He took one last look at Hurtfew Abbey and galloped away [Clarke, 2015, p. 923].

This experience is not only Childermass's, for a couple of pages later it is revealed that the whole of the English sky is undergoing the same process. "Time passed. It was impossible to say how much. The clocks had all turned to midnight. Every window shewed the black of Eternal Night and the unknown stars" (Clarke, 2015, p. 925). For Kant, the enduring image of the starry heavens above him reflected the eternal truth of the moral law within him. The symbolic gesture of removing those stars, of creating new constellations, is Clarke's affirmation of the hope that a new ethical era may be ready to dawn in England, one that will finally do away with the madness of its imperial past.

# References

Adorno, T.W., & Horkheimer, M., 2002. *Dialectic of Enlightenment: Philosophical Fragments.* Stanford: Stanford University Press.
Anonymous, 2014. *The Poetic Edda.* Oxford: Oxford University Press.
Armitage, D., 2004. *The Ideological Origins of the British Empire.* Cambridge: Cambridge University Press.
Armstrong, N., 2005. *How Novels Think: The Limits of British Individualism from 1719–1900.* New York: Columbia University Press.
Arnold, C., 2008. *Bedlam: London and Its Mad.* London: Pocket.
Austen, J., 2003. *Sense and Sensibility.* London: Penguin.
Austen, J., 2008. *Northanger Abbey, Lady Susan, The Watsons, Sanditon.* Oxford: Oxford University Press.
Bailey, M.D., 2007. *Magic and Superstition in Europe: A Concise History from Antiquity to the Present.* Lanham, MD: Rowman & Littlefield.
Baker, D., 2011. "History as Fantasy: Estranging the Past in *Jonathan Strange and Mr. Norell.*" *Otherness: Essays and Studies,* 2(1), pp. 1–16.
Bander, E., 2008. "Miss J. Austen, Jonathan Strange & Mr. Norrell." *Persuasions: The Jane Austen Journal On-Line,* Winter 29(1).
Barthes, R., 1972. *Mythologies.* New York: Farrar, Straus and Giroux.
Barthes, R., 1978. "The Death of the Author." In *Image-Music-Text.* New York: Hill & Wang, pp. 142–148.
Bede, 2011. *The Ecclesiastical History of the English People.* Mineola, NY: Dover Publications.
Begg, D., & Begg, E., 2008. *In Search of the Holy Grail and the Precious Blood: A Travellers' Guide.* Bloomington, IN: iUniverse.
Bennett, J., 2001. *The Enchantment of Modern Life: Attachments, Crossings, and Ethics.* Princeton: Princeton University Press.
Birns, N., 2020. "*Jonathan Strange & Mr Norrell,* the Magic of Sociality, and Radical Fantasy." *Humanities,* 9(4), p. 125.
Blake, W., 2004. *The Complete Poems.* London: Penguin.
Borowska-Szerszun, S., 2015. "The Interplay of the Domestic and the Uncanny in Susanna Clarke's *Jonathan Strange and Mr Norrell.*" *Crossroads: A Journal of English Studies,* Volume 9, pp. 4–12.
Braddon, M.E., 1998. *Lady Audley's Secret.* London: Penguin.
Brontë, C., 2006. *Jane Eyre.* London: Penguin.
Brown, P., 2012. "Gnostic Magic in *Jonathan Strange and Mr. Norell.*" *Journal of the Fantastic in the Arts,* 23(2), pp. 239–259.
Byatt, A.S., 1992. *The Virgin in the Garden.* New York: Vintage.
Byron, L., 2005. *Manfred: A Dramatic Poem.* In S.J. Wolfson & P.J. Manning, eds., *Selected Poems.* London: Penguin, pp. 463–506.

# References

Carr-Gomm, P., & Heygate, R., 2010. *The Book of English Magic*. New York: Overlook Press.
Carroll, L., 1998. *Alice's Adventures in Wonderland/Through the Looking-Glass and What Alice Found There*. London: Penguin.
Cervantes, M. d., 2000. *Don Quixote*. London: Penguin.
Churms, S.E., 2019. *Romanticism and Popular Magic: Poetry and the Cultures of the Occult in the 1790s*. Cham, Switzerland: Palgrave Macmillan.
Clarke, S., 2004. *The Susanna Clarke interview* [Interview] (24 September 2004).
Clarke, S., 2005a. *An Interview with Susanna Clarke* [Interview] (September 2005).
Clarke, S., 2005b. *The Three Susanna Clarkes* [Interview] (April 2005).
Clarke, S., 2007a. *Susanna Clarke, author of Jonathan Strange & Mr. Norrell* [Interview] (2007).
Clarke, S., 2007b. *The Ladies of Grace Adieu*. London: Bloomsbury.
Clarke, S., 2015. *Jonathan Strange and Mr. Norrell*. London: Bloomsbury.
Clarke, S., 2020. *Piranesi*. New York and London: Bloomsbury.
Coetzee, J.M., 1987. *Foe*. New York: Penguin.
Columbus, C., 1997. *The Book of Prophecies*. Berkeley: University of California Press.
Crowley, A., 1974. *The Book of Thoth*. York Beach, ME: Weiser.
Davies, O., 2003. *Popular Magic: Cunning Folk in English History*. London: Hambledon Continuum.
Davies, O., 2009. *Grimoires: A History of Magic Books*. Oxford: Oxford University Press.
Day, J.T., 1987. *Stendhal's Paper Mirror: Patterns of Self-Consciousness in His Novels*. New York: Peter Lang.
Dee, J., 1968. *The Perfect Arte of Navigation*. New York: Da Capo Press.
Defoe, D., 2007. *Robinson Crusoe*. Oxford: Oxford University Press.
Deleuze, G., 1989. Coldness and Cruelty. In: *Masochism: Coldness and Cruelty & Venus in Furs*. New York: Zone, pp. 7–138.
Derrida, J., 1978. "Cogito and the History of Madness." In *Writing and Difference*. London: Routledge, pp. 36–76.
Derrida, J., 1981. *Dissemination*. London: The Athlone Press.
Descartes, R., 2003. *Meditations and Other Metaphysical Writings*. London: Penguin.
Dirda, M., 2004. "Jonathan Strange and Mr. Norrell." *The Washington Post*, 5 September, p. BW15.
Doerr, R.B., 2016. "Summons, Prophecies, Possession and Madness: Intersections of Law and Magic in *Jonathan Strange and Mr. Norrell*." In D. Carpi & M. Leiboff, eds., *Fables of the Law: Fairy Tales in a Legal Context*. Berlin: Walter de Gruyter, pp. 379–418.
Dryden, J., 2001. *Selected Poems*. London: Penguin.
During, S., 2002. *Modern Enchantments: The Cultural Power of Secular Magic*. Cambridge: Harvard University Press.
Ebbatson, R., 1993. "'The Withered Arm' and History." *Critical Survey*, 5(2), pp. 131–136.
Erasmus, D., 1993. *Praise of Folly*. Harmondsworth: Penguin.
Evangelou, A., 2017. *Philosophizing Madness from Nietzsche to Derrida*. Cham, Switzerland: Palgrave Macmillan.
Feingold, M., 2013. "'And Knowledge Shall Be Increased': Millenarianism and the Advancement of Learning Revisited." *The Seventeenth Century*, 28(4), pp. 363–393.
Felman, S., 2003. *Writing and Madness: Literature/Philosophy/Psychoanalysis*. Palo Alto: Stanford University Press.
Flaubert, G., 1976. *Bouvard and Pécuchet*. Harmondsworth: Penguin.
Foucault, M., 1984. "What Is Enlightenment?" In P. Rabinow, ed., *The Foucault Reader*. New York: Pantheon, pp. 32–50.
Foucault, M., 1994. *The Order of Things: An Archaeology of the Human Sciences*. New York: Vintage.

# References

Foucault, M., 2006. *History of Madness*. London: Routledge.
Frazer, J. G., 1981. *The Golden Bough*. New York: Gramercy.
French, P., 2002. *John Dee: The World of the Elizabethan Magus*. New York: Routledge.
Fromm, E., 1994. *Escape from Reason*. New York: Henry Holt and Company.
Gildas, 2002. *The Ruin of Britain and Other Works*. Revised ed. London: Phillimore.
Greenfeld, L., 2013. *Mind, Modernity, Madness: The Impact of Culture on Human Experience*. Cambridge: Harvard University Press.
Greenwood, S., 2009. *The Anthropology of Magic*. Oxford: Berg.
Hacking, I., 2006. Foreword. In *History of Madness*. New York: Routledge, pp. ix–xii.
Hanegraaff, W.J., 2012. *Esotericism and the Academy: Rejected Knowledge in Western Culture*. Cambridge: Cambridge University Press.
Hardy, T., 1999. *The Withered Arm and Other Stories*. London: Penguin.
Harrison, P., 2015. *The Territories of Science and Religion*. Chicago: University of Chicago Press.
Heng, G., 2003. *Empire of Magic: Medieval Romance and the Politics of Cultural Fantasy*. New York: Columbia University Press.
Henry, B.W., 1972. "John Dee, Humphrey Llwyd, and the Name 'British Empire.'" *Huntington Library Quarterly*, 35(2), pp. 189–190.
Henry, J., 2017. *Knowledge Is Power: How Magic, the Government and an Apocalyptic Vision Helped Francis Bacon to Create Modern Science*. London: Icon Books.
Hodgman, J., 2004. "Susanna Clarke's Magic Book." *The New York Times*, 1 August, p. 20.
Hoiem, E., 2008. "The Fantasy of Talking Back: Susanna Clarke's Historical Present in *Jonathan Strange and Mr. Norrell*." *Strange Horizons*, 27 October.
Hoyle, V., 2006. "*The Ladies of Grace Adieu* by Susanna Clarke." *Strange Horizons*, 20 November.
Hutton, R., 1993. *The Pagan Religions of the Ancient British Isles: Their Nature and Legacy*. Oxford: Blackwell.
Iliopoulos, J., 2017. *The History of Reason in the Age of Madness*. London: Bloomsbury.
Irigaray, L., 1993. *Je, Tu, Nous: Toward a Culture of Difference*. New York: Routledge.
Jones, G.M., 2017. *Magic's Reason: An Anthropology of Analogy*. Chicago: University of Chicago Press.
Jonson, B., 2004. *Volpone and Other Plays*. London: Penguin.
Josephson-Storm, J.Ā., 2017. *The Myth of Disenchantment: Magic, Modernity, and the Birth of the Human Sciences*. Chicago: University of Chicago Press.
Kafka, F., 2009. *The Trial*. Oxford: Oxford University Press.
Kant, I., 1997. *Critique of Practical Reason*. Cambridge: Cambridge University Press.
Kantorowicz, E.H., 1997. *The King's Two Bodies: A Study in Mediaeval Political Theology*. Princeton: Princeton University Press.
Kieckhefer, R., 2014. *Magic in the Middle Ages*. Second ed. Cambridge: Cambridge University Press.
Lacan, J., 2006. *Écrits: The First Complete Edition in English*. New York: W.W. Norton & Company.
Laclos, P.C. d., 1961. *Les Liaisons Dangereuses*. Harmondsworth: Penguin.
Laity, K.A., 2018. "The Unlikely Milliner & The Magician of Threadneedle-Street." *Mythlore: A Journal of J.R.R. Tolkien, C.S. Lewis, Charles Williams, and Mythopoeic Literature*, 36(2), pp. 215–229.
Lawrence-Mathers, A., 2012. *The True History of Merlin the Magician*. New Haven: Yale University Press.
Le Guin, U.K., 1990. *The Earthsea Trilogy*. Harmondsworth: Penguin.
Lewis, C.S., 2010. *Prince Caspian: The Return to Narnia*. London: HarperCollins.
Lewis, C.S., 2010. *The Lion, the Witch and the Wardrobe*. London: HarperCollins.

# References

Locke, J., 1959. *An Essay Concerning Human Understanding*. Mineola, NY: Dover.
Louv, J., 2018. *John Dee and the Empire of Angels: Enochian Magic and the Occult Roots of the Modern World*. Rochester, VT: Inner Traditions.
Malory, T., 2004. *Le Morte d'Arthur*. London: Penguin.
Marlowe, C., 2003. *The Complete Plays*. London: Penguin.
Martin, R., 1988. "Truth, Power, Self: An Interview with Michel Foucault." In L. H. Martin, H. Gutman & P. H. Hutton, eds., *Technologies of the Self*. London: Tavistock Publications, pp. 9–15.
Mauss, M., & Hubert, H., 2001. *A General Theory of Magic*. New York: Routledge.
Milton, J., 2003. *Paradise Lost*. London: Penguin.
Milton, J., 2018. *The History of Britain, That Part Especially now Called England: From the First Traditional Beginning Continued to the Norman Conquest*. Franklin Classics Trade Press.
Monmouth, G. o., 1973. *Life of Merlin*. Cardiff: University of Wales Press.
Monmouth, G. o., 1977. *The History of the Kings of Britain*. Harmondsworth: Penguin.
Monod, P.K., 2013. *Solomon's Secret Arts: The Occult in the Age of Enlightenment*. New Haven: Yale University Press.
Murry, J.M., 1971. *William Blake*. New York: Haskell House.
Owen, A., 2004. *The Place of Enchantment: British Occultism and the Culture of the Modern*. Chicago: University of Chicago Press.
Padel, O.J., 2019. "Cornwall and the Matter of Britain." In C. Lloyd-Morgan & E. Poppe, eds., *Arthur in the Celtic Languages: The Arthurian Legend in Celtic Literatures and Traditions*. Cardiff: University of Wales Press, pp. 263–280.
Paracelsus, 1990. *Essential Writings*. Wellingborough, Northamptonshire: Crucible.
Plato, 2005. *Phaedrus*. London: Penguin.
Porter, R., 2000. *Enlightenment: Britain and the Creation of the Modern World*. London: Allen Lane.
Porter, R., 2002. *Madness: A Brief History*. Oxford and New York: Oxford University Press.
Robert-Houdin, J.-E., 1859. *Memoirs of Robert-Houdin: Ambassador, Author, and Conjuror*. London: Chapman and Hall.
Rudgley, R., 2018. *The Return of Odin: The Modern Renaissance of Pagan Imagination*. Third ed. Rochester, VT: Inner Traditions.
Sade, M. d., 2012. *Justine, or The Misfortunes of Virtue*. Oxford: Oxford University Press.
Salkeld, D., 1993. *Madness and Drama in the Age of Shakespeare*. Manchester: Manchester University Press.
Sanghera, S., 2021. *Empireland: How Imperialism Has Shaped Modern Britain*. London: Viking.
Savage, C., 2015. *Crows: Encounters with the Wise Guys of the Avian World*. 10th Anniversary ed. Vancouver: Greystone Books.
Scanlan, P.X., 2020. *Slave Empire: How Slavery Built Modern Britain*. London: Robinson.
Schuler, R.M., 2004. "Magic Mirrors in *Richard II*." *Comparative Drama*, 38(2/3), pp. 151–181.
Scott, W., 1985. *Waverley*. London: Penguin.
Scull, A., 2015. *Madness in Civilization: A Cultural History of Insanity, from the Bible to Freud, from the Madhouse to Modern Medicine*. Princeton: Princeton University Press.
Shakespeare, W., 1998. *The Oxford Shakespeare: Hamlet*. Oxford: Oxford University Press.
Shakespeare, W., 1998. *The Tempest*. New York: Signet.
Shakespeare, W., 1999. *A Midsummer Night's Dream: Texts and Contexts*. Boston: Bedford/St Martin's.

## References

Shakespeare, W., 2001. *King Lear.* Oxford: Oxford University Press.
Shakespeare, W., 2008. *The Oxford Shakespeare: Henry IV, Part 1.* Oxford: Oxford University Press.
Shakespeare, W., 2008. *The Oxford Shakespeare: The Tragedy of Macbeth.* Oxford: Oxford University Press.
Shakespeare, W., 2011. *Richard II.* Oxford: Oxford University Press.
Shakespeare, W., 2014. *As You Like It: Texts and Contexts.* Boston: Bedford/St. Martin's.
Shelley, M., 1998. *Frankenstein, or The Modern Prometheus.* Oxford: Oxford University Press.
Showalter, E., 1987. *The Female Malady: Women, Madness, and English Culture, 1830–1980.* Harmondsworth: Penguin.
Smith, A., 1999. *The Wealth of Nations.* London: Penguin.
Spenser, E., 1987. *The Faerie Queene.* Harmondsworth: Penguin.
Stendhal, 2002. *The Red and the Black.* London: Penguin.
Styers, R., 2004. *Making Magic: Religion, Magic, and Science in the Modern World.* Oxford: Oxford University Press.
Swift, J., 2008. *A Tale of a Tub and Other Works.* Oxford: Oxford University Press.
Taliesin, 2019. *The Book of Taliesin: Poems of Warfare and Praise in an Enchanted Britain.* London: Penguin.
Tennyson, A.L., 2007. *Selected Poems.* London: Penguin.
Thomas, K., 2003. *Religion and the Decline of Magic: Studies in Popular Beliefs in Sixteenth and Seventeenth Century England.* London: Penguin.
Tolkien, J.R.R., 2002. *The Lord of the Rings.* New York: Houghton Mifflin Harcourt.
Tylor, E.B., 2016. *Primitive Culture.* Mineola, NY: Dover.
Virgil, 2003. *The Aeneid.* London: Penguin.
Virgil, 2009. *The Eclogues/Georgics.* Oxford: Oxford University Press.
Wales, G. o., 2004. *The Journey Through Wales/The Description of Wales.* London: Penguin.
Walker, J.M., 1998. *Medusa's Mirrors: Spenser, Shakespeare, Milton, and the Metamorphosis of the Female Self.* Newark: University of Delaware Press.
Wallis, R. J., 2017. "Witchcraft and Magic in the Age of Anthropology." In O. Davies, ed., *The Oxford Illustrated History of Witchcraft and Magic.* Oxford: Oxford University Press, pp. 225–252.
Watt, I., 2000. *The Rise of the Novel: Studies in Defoe, Richardson and Fielding.* London: Pimlico.
Weber, M., 1946. "Science as a Vocation." IN *From Max Weber: Essays in Sociology.* New York: Oxford University Press, pp. 12n–156.
Weber, M., 2001. *The Protestant Ethic and the Spirit of Capitalism.* London: Routledge.
Webster, C., 1982. *From Paracelsus to Newton: Magic and the Making of Modern Science.* Cambridge: Cambridge University Press.
Webster, J., 1995. *Three Plays.* London: Penguin.
Weiner, D.B., 2008. "The Madman in the Light of Reason. Enlightenment Psychiatry: Part II. Alienists, Treatises, and the Psychologic Approach in the Era of Pinel." In E. R. Wallace IV & J. Gach, eds., *History of Psychiatry and Medical Psychology.* New York: Springer, pp. 281–303.
White, T.H., 2010. *The Sword in the Stone.* London: HarperCollins.
Wilby, E., 2005. *Cunning Folk and Familiar Spirits: Shamanistic Visionary Traditions in Early Modern British Witchcraft and Magic.* Eastbourne, UK: Sussex Academic Press.
Wollstonecraft, M., 2004. *A Vindication of the Rights of Women.* London: Penguin.
Wollstonecraft, M., & Shelley, M., 2004. *Mary/Maria/Matilda.* London: Penguin.
Wyss, J., 1991. *The Swiss Family Robinson.* Oxford: Oxford University Press.

# References

Yates, F.A., 1975. *Astraea: The Imperial Theme in the Sixteenth Century.* London: Pimlico.
Yates, F.A., 1991. *Giordano Bruno and the Hermetic Tradition.* Chicago: University of Chicago Press.
Yates, F.A., 2001. *The Occult Philosophy in the Elizabethan Age.* New York: Routledge.
Yates, F.A., 2002. *The Rosicrucian Enlightenment.* Abingdon: Routledge.
Youngquist, P., 1994. "Vision, Madness, Myth and William Blake." In B. M. Rieger, ed., *Dionysus in Literature: Essays on Literary Madness.* Bowling Green, OH: Bowling Green State University Popular Press, pp. 113–132.
Ziolkowski, J., 1990. "The Nature of Prophecy in Geoffrey of Monmouth's *Vita Merlini*." In J. L. Kugel, ed., *Poetry and Prophecy: The Beginnings of a Literary Tradition.* Ithaca: Cornell University Press, pp. 151–162.
Žižek, S., 2014. "Cogito, Madness, and Religion: Derrida, Foucault, and Then Lacan." In: C. Davis, M. Pound & C. Crockett, eds. *Theology After Lacan: The Passion for the Real.* Eugene, OR: Cascade, pp. 19–33.

# Index

Adorno, Theodor 117–120, 122, 154
alchemy 12–13, 18, 20, 30, 35, 80, 103
Amis, Martin 5
anthropology 92, 105–113, 134–135
Apollo 55
Argentine magicians 23
Armitage, David 21
Armstrong, Nancy 90
Arnold, Catharine 73, 98–100
Arthur, King 2, 6, 9, 13, 17–18, 20–21, 34, 59, 63, 88, 92, 97, 101
artificial myth 78–79, 82–83, 85–86, 88, 122
Astraea 17–18
astrology 80, 145, 147, 157–158
Atwood, Margaret 5
Aureate magicians 1, 23, 44–45, 49, 80–81, 124, 138
Austen, Jane 25, 46, 58, 60, 63, 82, 135–136
awen 11–12, 55

Bacon, Francis 69, 151–152
Bacon, Roger 28
Bailey, Michael D. 36
Baker, Daniel 47, 57–61
Bander, Elaine 46
Barthes, Roland 51, 53, 76–79, 82
Beckford, William 89
Bede 14
Bedlam 73–74, 98
Bennett, Jane 80–82
Birns, Nicholas 3, 24–25, 105
Black, Stephen 43, 64–65, 101–103, 105–106, 112, 126, 138, 151
Blake, William 148–151
books of magic *see* grimoire
Borowska-Szerszun, Sylwia 46–47, 56–58
Braddon, Mary Elizabeth 76
Brant, Sebastian 130
Brexit 1

British Empire 1–2, 18–21, 25, 63, 69, 83, 102, 157
Brontë, Charlotte 58, 76
Brown, Paula 92–94
Byatt, A.S. 2
Byron, Lord 25, 31, 33, 57, 69, 126, 152–153

Carr-Gomm, Philip 17, 19, 30, 35, 64
Carroll, Lewis 128, 137, 140
Cervantes, Miguel de 34, 100, 135–136
Charles II 17, 67–68, 94
Cheyne, George 74
Childermass, John 33, 43–44, 50–51, 53, 55, 124, 127, 152–153, 156–158
Christianity 12, 21, 36, 38, 40, 48, 130, 149
Churms, Stephanie Elizabeth 41
class 3, 7–8, 26, 29, 38–41, 44, 56, 65, 99, 114, 124–125
Coetzee, J.M. 47
Coleridge, Samuel Taylor 41, 137
colonialism *see* imperialism
Columbus, Christopher 19–21
Copernicus 145
Crowley, Aleister 52
Crowley, John 5
cunning-folk 7, 39–42, 48

Darwin, Charles 107
Davies, Owen 37–41, 47–49, 54
Day, James T. 85
Dee, John 2, 16–21, 71–72, 95–96, 101
Defoe, Daniel 47
Deleuze, Gilles 143–144
Derrida, Jacques 52, 101, 128, 132–133
Descartes, René 101, 128, 131–134, 156
Dickens, Charles 58
Dirda, Michael 5
disenchantment 27–29, 38, 42, 79–83, 109, 111, 117, 121, 145, 151–154
Doerr, Roxanne Barbara 136–137

165

# Index

double 25, 32, 58, 73, 82, 86, 88, 91–92, 97, 102, 111, 113, 118, 121, 126–131, 133, 136, 142, 155
Drake, Francis 19
Drawlight, Christopher 69, 87, 146
Dryden, John 17
During, Simon 35–36, 110–114

Ebbatson, Roger 40
Eco, Umberto 5
Edward the Confessor 94
Edward III 67
Eliot, T.S. 92
Elizabeth I 16–21, 63, 69–70, 91–92, 94–95
Endless Night 148, 150, 158
English malady 74–75, 98, 140, 142, 157
Englishness 30–35, 38, 56, 64–65, 105–106, 109, 149, 157–158
Enlightenment 23, 27, 41, 80, 99, 101, 113–114, 116–122, 134–135
Erasmus 130–131, 133
Evangelou, Angelos 131

fairies 1, 8, 11, 32, 37, 39–41, 43–44, 70–71, 81, 83, 88, 100–103, 105, 112, 125–127, 137–138, 141, 152
Feingold, Mordechai 152
Felman, Shoshana 72, 86, 132–133, 135, 154–155
Flaubert, Gustave 79
Foucault, Michel 45, 51, 101, 127–136, 151
Frazer, Sir James 56, 92–93, 100, 107–108
French, Peter 71
French Revolution 41, 90, 99, 148
Freud, Sigmund 92
Fromm, Erich 116–117, 120–121

Galileo 80
gentleman with the thistledown hair 37, 54, 89, 101–103, 112, 125–126, 146
Geoffrey of Monmouth 9–17, 101, 145, 147, 157
George III 22, 25, 67–68, 96–103, 124
Gerald of Wales 10–11
Gildas 14
Gothic 37, 46, 49, 57–59, 82, 89
Graves, Robert 92
Greatrakes, Valentine 37
Greenfeld, Liah 74
Greenwood, Susan 107–108, 128–129, 152
Greysteel, Miss Flora 31, 68, 88–89, 139
grimoire 37, 41, 47–49
Gwyn, Nell 67

Hacking, Ian 128, 132
Hanegraaff, Wouter J. 36
Hardy, Thomas 40
Harrison, Peter 44–45
Heng, Geraldine 2
Henry, John 151–152
Henry I 14
Henry VII 94
Henry VIII 16
Heygate, Richard 17, 19, 30, 35, 64
Hodgman, John 5
Hogarth, William 98
Hoiem, Elizabeth 64–65
Homer 118
Hood, Robin 63
Horkheimer, Max 117–120, 122, 154
Horney, Karen 116
Hoyle, Virginia 141–142
Hutton, Ronald 30

Iliopoulos, John 134–135
imperialism 1–3, 15–16, 18–22, 48, 56–57, 59–60, 64–69, 82–83, 90, 93–94, 99, 102, 105–117, 120, 149–150, 157–158
Irigaray, Luce 77

Jones, Graham M. 106, 110–111, 113–115
Jonson, Ben 69
Josephson-Storm, Jason 27–29, 120–121, 154
Joyce, James 92

Kafka, Franz 144
Kant, Immanuel 134–135, 143–144, 148, 150, 158
Kantorowicz, Ernst 95–96, 99
Kieckhefer, Richard 36, 54
King's Evil 93–94, 97
King's Letters 50, 54

Lacan, Jacques 100
Laclos, Pierre Choderlos de 126
*The Ladies of Grace Adieu* 2–3, 42, 124, 141–142
Laity, K.A. 52–53, 155
Lascelles, Henry 49–50, 158
Lawrence, D.H. 92
Lawrence-Mathers, Anne 12–16, 147–148
Le Guin, Ursula 126
Lewis, C.S. 23–24, 46, 57, 64
Lewis, Matthew 89
Locke, John 50
Louv, Jason 18–21
Lovecraft, H.P. 92

# Index

madness 1–3, 11, 21–22, 28, 55, 67–68, 70, 72–76, 83, 86, 97–101, 112, 120, 123–142, 147, 150–152, 156–158
Malory, Thomas 9
Marlowe, Christopher 2, 69, 71–72
Mary I 16, 18
Mauss, Marcel 107
Merlin 2, 6, 8–18, 21–22, 37, 55–56, 59, 69–70, 73, 92, 145, 147–148
Milton, John 100, 149–150
Mirandola, Giovanni Pico della 37
mirror 48, 60–61, 85–98, 103, 127, 130–131, 133, 137–139, 146
Monod, Paul Kléber 38–39
Mozart, Wolfgang Amadeus 137
Murry, John Middleton 148
myth 2, 7–18, 20–22, 24–25, 27, 30, 34, 44, 46–47, 50, 52–57, 59–64, 66–68, 70, 74–86, 91–93, 96–97, 100–101, 106, 112, 119–122, 128–129, 149–154, 157

Napoleon 16, 24, 30–31, 57, 66–67, 89, 99
Napoleonic Wars 3, 7, 22, 24, 30, 57, 99
Newton, Isaac 45, 80, 145
Nietzsche, Friedrich 28, 78, 128
Noah 93, 97, 149
Norfolk, Lawrence 5
Norrell, Gilbert 1, 6–9, 16–17, 23, 26, 29–30, 33, 37, 41–42, 44, 48–50, 65, 67, 75, 81, 83, 85–87, 89, 123–126, 137, 139, 141–142, 144, 152–153, 155

Odin 54–56
Owen, Alex 25–26

Padel, Oliver J. 34
Paracelsus 45
pastiche 3, 25, 46, 58, 60
Peake, Mervyn 5
Pinel, Philippe 75
*Piranesi* 2–3, 44
Plato 52
Pole, Lady 37, 43, 76, 88, 125–127, 151
Pole, Walter 7, 102, 138–139
Porter, Roy 74–75, 98
prophecy 10–17, 36, 55, 70, 100, 123, 145–149, 155, 158

racism 99, 102–109, 111, 113, 115, 120, 149, 158
Radcliffe, Ann 89
raven 34, 54–55, 70
Raven King 7–9, 23, 28, 30, 32–34, 37, 42, 44, 49, 50, 53–55, 67, 79–83, 91, 93, 96–97, 123–124, 126, 144, 146–147, 152–153, 155
return of magic 7–8, 22–31, 38, 42, 82–83, 93, 144, 146–147, 152–153, 157
Robert-Fleury, Tony 75
Robert-Houdin, Jean-Eugène 106, 110, 113–115, 118
Rudgley, Richard 55–56

sacrifice 118–119
Sade, Marquis de 144
Salkeld, Duncan 73
Sanghera, Sathnam 1
Savage, Candace 54–55
Scanlan, Padraic X. 1
Schiller, Friedrich 29
Schuler, Robert M. 95–96
Scot, Reginald 48
Scott, Walter 8, 90
scrying 146
Scull, Andrew 123
secular magic 110–115
Segundus, John 16, 37, 58, 75, 124
Shakespeare, William 63, 69–74, 94–95, 97
Shelley, Mary 90
Showalter, Elaine 75–76
simulacrum 86, 88
slavery 1, 24–25, 48, 60, 83, 99, 102–103, 117–118, 149, 157
Smith, Adam 66
sovereignty 3, 21, 24, 91, 99, 102, 135
Spenser, Edmund 2, 15, 17, 71–72, 91–94
Spinoza, Baruch de 28
Starecross Hall 75, 124, 127
stars 143–150, 157; *see also* astrology
Stendhal 85–86, 89
Stephen of Blois 14–15
Strange, Arabella 76, 88–89, 121–122, 124, 126, 141, 146
Strange, Jonathan 1, 7–9, 11, 16–17, 22, 26, 28, 31–33, 42–43, 49, 64–65, 67–69, 81–82, 85–89, 99–101, 121–126, 136–142, 146–148, 152–153
Styers, Randall 26, 108–109, 112
Swift, Jonathan 73–74

Taliesin 11–12, 148
tarot 52, 155–156
Tennyson, Lord Alfred 9, 88–89
Thomas, Keith 28, 36, 38, 41, 70–71, 93–94, 129, 145
Thoth 52

167

# Index

Tolkien, J.R.R. 5, 24–25, 46, 64, 126
Tuke, William 75–76
Turner, J.M.W. 92
Tylor, Edward Burnett 106–108, 110

unreason *see* madness

Venice 31, 33, 68–69, 88, 138–139, 146
Verrio, Antonio 67–68
Victoria I 98
Vinculus 6–7, 10, 37, 45–47, 49–51, 53–55, 65, 82, 105–106, 123, 152–153, 155
Virgil 17, 91–92

Walker, Julia M. 91–92, 95
Wallis, Robert J. 107
Watt, Ian 50
Weber, Max 25, 27–28, 38, 79–82, 111
Webster, Charles 45

Webster, John 73
Weiner, Dora B. 75
Wellington, Lord 8–9, 30, 57, 137–139
White, T.H. 5, 9
Wilby, Emma 41–42
Wintertowne, Miss Emma *see* Pole, Lady
witchcraft 39, 41, 48, 70, 107–108, 111, 130
Wollstonecraft, Mary 76
writing 9, 13–16, 43–61, 70–72, 90, 106, 146, 152, 156–157
Wyss, Johann David 47

Yates, Frances A. 17–18, 20, 71–72, 80
Yeats, W.B. 92
Youngquist, Paul 150

Ziolkowski, Jan 11
Žižek, Slavoj 132

www.ingramcontent.com/pod-product-compliance
Lightning Source LLC
Chambersburg PA
CBHW032047300426
44117CB00009B/1225